THE GREGS OF
QUARRY BANK MILL

This is a study of an important family business, set firmly within the wider context of English society during the period of industrialisation. Established at a time of predominantly small-scale business organisation, the firm of Samuel Greg & Co. soon emerged as one of the very few giants within the cotton industry, and the reasons for this rapid growth provide valuable insights into the nature of English industrial activity during the Industrial Revolution. Indeed the very factors that made for expansion of Samuel Greg and Co. explain, paradoxically, why large-scale firms were so unusual.

The Gregs' strength was however, short-lived. The shifting competitive environment of the industry, the difficulties of change in archaic water-powered mills, and the diverse personalities of the founder's sons, all contributed to the decline of the firm from 1840 onwards. In an age when comparatively few businesses survived for more than one or two generations, such lengthy decline enables the author to analyse the peculiar problems posed by technological obsolescence and managerial inertia during industrialisation.

Although *The Gregs of Quarry Bank Mill* views the workings of a business within the economy as a whole, the importance of personality is not forgotten, and its impact upon the conduct of a family business is graphically revealed by the varied abilities of individual Gregs. At Styal itself the Greg family can be numbered amongst the first factory colonisers, and enjoyed a close relationship with the Quarry Bank workforce, later to inspire the Utopian experiments of Samuel Greg Junior at Bollington. As an influential part of a close-knit community of non-conformist mercantile families, the prominence of the Greg family makes them an ideal vehicle for an intensive analysis of society and politics among the manufacturing sector in the eighteenth and nineteenth centuries.

THE GREGS OF
QUARRY BANK MILL

The rise and decline of a
family firm, 1750–1914

MARY B. ROSE

Lecturer in Economics at the University of Lancaster

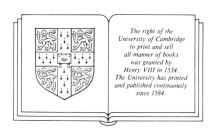

The right of the
University of Cambridge
to print and sell
all manner of books
was granted by
Henry VIII in 1534.
The University has printed
and published continuously
since 1584.

CAMBRIDGE UNIVERSITY PRESS

Cambridge
London   New York   New Rochelle
Melbourne   Sydney

Published by the Press Syndicate of the University of Cambridge
The Pitt Building, Trumpington Street, Cambridge CB2 1RP
32 East 57th Street, New York, NY 10022, USA
10 Stamford Road, Oakleigh, Melbourne 3166, Australia

First published 1986

Printed in Great Britain at the University Press, Cambridge

British Library cataloguing in publication data

Rose, Mary B.
The Gregs of Quarry Bank Mill: the rise and decline of a
family firm, 1750–1914.
1. Greg *(Family)*
I. Title   II. Quarry Bank Mill Trust
338.7'67721'0922   CS439.G715/

Library of Congress Cataloguing-in-Publication Data

Rose, Mary B.
The Gregs of Quarry Bank Mill.
Bibliography: p.
1. Quarry Bank Mill – History. 2. Cotton textile industry –
Great Britain – History. 3. Greg family.
I. Title.
HD9881.9.Q3R66 1987338.7'67721'0942493   85-29113

ISBN 0 521 32382 7 hard covers
(Paperback edition for sale by Quarry Bank Mill Trust only)

CE

To R. P. G, A. T. G and A. C. G,
the sons of Ernest William Greg

CONTENTS

PHOTOGRAPHS

FIGURES

TABLES

ACKNOWLEDGEMENTS

That this book has been so long in appearing is a source of deep embarrassment to me. It can only be attributed to the pressures of a new job, procrastination and occasional loss of hope. Inevitably over the years I have received invaluable help from a wide range of sources, both as a graduate student and more recently in the direct preparation of this manuscript.

All errors and omissions are, of course, mine. However, I owe a great deal to my colleagues in the Department of Economics at the University of Lancaster. Perhaps my greatest debt is to the late Dr Harry Dutton who persuaded me that I could write the book. Gratitude is also due to Mr Oliver Westall, whose painstaking perusal of the first and subsequent drafts gave me untold headaches but guaranteed that a better book was written. Thanks are also due to Mr John King and Dr Penny Summerfield for the helpful comments they made on individual chapters. I am also grateful to Dr Sheila Marriner, University of Liverpool, for the interest she has shown over the years and for many helpful suggestions. I should like to thank Dr Douglas Farnie, University of Manchester, who supervised my PhD and who has made valuable comments on the present manuscript. The students of Economics 308, University of Lancaster, from 1978 to 1984 also deserve a mention, for they were the initial recipients of many of the ideas in this book. I am also grateful to the University of Lancaster for granting me sabbatical leave, enabling me to write the book, and especially to Mr Oliver Westall and Dr John Channon, who shouldered my teaching burdens at a very difficult time.

The staff of the many libraries and archives I have used over the years have shown unfailing patience and are too numerous all to be mentioned. Of especial help was Miss J. Ayton and the staff of the Archives Department at Manchester Central Library. In addition archivists at the Cheshire Record Office, Liverpool University Library and the City Library, Liverpool, were of great assistance. To the National Trust and to Quarry Bank Mill Development Trust I am eternally grateful for granting me access to the vast collection of material at Styal during the 1970s. Mr W. Salt (then of Greg Brothers) was also very generous in providing me with a room to work in and endless cups of tea, as well as access to the records in his possession. Without the Greg family themselves and their continued interest in the project as a whole, it is possible I might have lost heart. Both Mr. A. C. Greg and Mrs S. B. L. Jacks have been most supportive and helpful throughout.

I owe a great debt to the Director of Quarry Bank Mill Museum, Mr David Sekers, for supporting my proposal to write the book, and to the present museum staff, especially Mr Nigel Nixon, for their help in collecting the photographs for the text. All photographs are from Quarry Bank Mill's collection and are reproduced with their permission.

Great thanks are due to my mother, Sheila Kozlowski, for typing what must have seemed like innumerable drafts of the manuscript and for a superhuman attention to detail. I am grateful to Mrs Clare Coxon and Dr John Channon for help with proof reading. Finally, untold thanks are due to Tony Breakell for constant patience, support and enthusiasm during my sabbatical in 1984 and subsequently.

July 1985   M. B. ROSE

ABBREVIATIONS

AHR	*American Historical Review*
BH	*Business History*
CRO	Cheshire County Record Office
DCL	Derby City Library
EHR	*English Historical Review*
EcHR	*Economic History Review*
EJ	*Economic Journal*
JEH	*Journal of Economic History*
JRL	John Rylands Library
LaCL	Lancaster City Library
LCL	Liverpool City Library
LUL	Liverpool University Library
MCL	Manchester Central Library
QB	Quarry Bank Collection
PP	Parliamentary Papers
PRO	Public Record Office

INTRODUCTION

I

Cotton manufacturing, an exotic transplant into Britain, has captured the imagination of commentators and historians for generations. For a little over a century after 1770 it thrived, nourished by the enterprise of a close-knit commercial community and the abundant supply of cheap labour which accompanies poverty. Growing markets at home and, more especially, overseas fostered continued expansion for much of the nineteenth century. Lancashire where, by 1821, 35 per cent of the population were employed in the cotton trade, became the 'first industrial society', with Liverpool and Manchester dominating commercial life. Such was the overwhelming impression made by the cotton industry that, for many years, it was believed that it alone fuelled the industrial revolution. More recently, its contribution to economic development in the nineteenth century has been questioned and its position as the 'leading sector' in the industrial revolution challenged. A more realistic view is to be welcomed, for it placed the industry in perspective. Its fascination as the first factory industry, however, remains.

The industrial pioneers of the eighteenth century – the Arkwrights, the Strutts, the Darbys and the Wedgwoods – once peopled economic history. Their endeavours were believed to have created the industrial revolution. This obsession with personality has, however, given way to broader explanations of the trends of development. Business history, nevertheless, retains a prominent position, since case studies give invaluable insight into the management methods, labour relations and general business organisation of earlier phases of development. Moreover, macro-economic change is composed of micro-economic developments. The firms studied are often atypical, for many disappeared leaving little documentary evidence. Nevertheless, pro-

1

vided it is remembered that successful firms *were* unusual, their histories provide invaluable insight into the business environment and society of their time.

II

The Gregs are a fascinating family. Involved in the cotton industry for nearly two hundred years, they showed exceptional tenacity. Theirs is a story of a meteoric rise followed by a gradual decline into comparative obscurity. It is not, however, a 'rags to riches' fable. It was as a wealthy young man, in an established firm, that Samuel Greg began creating his business empire. Nor did the family sink into poverty after their industrial peak had been reached. For generations, no other Greg matched Samuel's business success and energy but, with few exceptions, the family remained comparatively wealthy.

The story of Quarry Bank Mill spans two centuries. It was Samuel Greg's first mill and opened in 1784. Now it is the home of a thriving textile museum. For many of Quarry Bank's thousands of modern visitors, it is far removed from their image of a cotton mill. In place of the grime, smoke and ugliness of an urban environment, they find an elegant building set in a deep, wooded valley beside an attractive Georgian house. Yet it was in just such countless similar settings that the industrial revolution began. Powered by water, rather than steam, early mills were built in the countryside, their owners importing the necessary labour, often from poorhouses. It is this which makes Quarry Bank such an intriguing window on the early industrial revolution. Moreover, through a study of its development and that of the other Greg mills in the nineteenth century, the problems of the early businessman are revealed.

As the history of a family business, this book traces the reactions and policies of five generations of Gregs, against the backcloth of a changing and maturing economy and society. The Gregs are interesting in their own right. The family has produced not only cotton magnates but politicians, literary commentators and mineralogists. Examined in isolation, their history would be meaningless. They were the products of the changing world in which they lived. A glance at their family tree shows their links with many of the leaders of business and commerce. To understand their lives is to understand something of life in the higher echelons of commercial society in Georgian and Victorian England.

The book spans 150 years of a cotton firm. It traces its earliest beginnings in eighteenth-century Lancashire and the movement from the domestic system when Quarry Bank was founded. The period following the Napoleonic Wars was a golden age for Samuel Greg and Company. New mills were purchased and Quarry Bank expanded to make the firm one of the giant businesses of the age. This pre-eminence was short lived. After the founder's death in 1834, the empire began to disintegrate, its focus lost. The name of Greg remained in the cotton industry but no longer in the vanguard. In an era when small firms were more typical, it is intriguing to discover how and why a large firm emerged and why its survival as a relative giant was short-lived.

By the mid-nineteenth century, the firm reached maturity and expansion slowed down. Some mills were sold, but Quarry Bank for some years thrived and Albert Mill, Reddish, was built. The so-called 'cotton famine' during the American Civil War had its effect, and the 1860s were a period of survival rather than prosperity. There followed four decades of varied fortunes. The firm, like the industry in which it operated, faced serious competition. Response at Albert Mill was positive, but Quarry Bank limped through the last years of the century, a pathetic relic of a bygone age.

Yet, in the late nineteenth and early twentieth centuries, the Gregs re-emerged at the forefront of the cotton industry. Both Arthur and his nephew, Ernest William Greg (grandson and great-grandson of Samuel), had highly successful careers heading Chadwicks, the sewing cotton giants. Henry Philips Greg (another great-grandson), was responsible for saving Albert Mill from obscurity, and for a while after the First World War it led the field in fancy yarn production.

Quarry Bank somehow survived until 1959 and the Gregs remained in the industry until 1963, nearly two hundred years after Samuel entered the trade. Such a long connection is almost unparalleled in the history of an industry which saw numerous and regular failures. This is what makes the firm such a useful window through which to view the rise and fall of the cotton industry.

The study of business in the nineteenth century is more than just an analysis of profit and loss, turnover and market trends; it is the study of personality. Like the Gregs, firms were comparatively small family affairs, operating in a close-knit environment where contact and personal knowledge counted for everything. It was the reactions of individuals to changing conditions and their standing within the business community which, for the most part, determined the firm's success. Thus, unlike the modern business corporations where personalities sometimes seem to be lost within a morass of bureaucracy, the nineteenth-century businessman emerges vividly.

It is as employers that the Gregs are best known. During the nineteenth century they were variously praised as model employers and castigated for 'making slaves of their operatives' via the cottage system and for continued use of parish apprentices. The factory colony at Styal, little changed since the nineteenth cenury, remains a constant reminder of the Gregs' attitude to their workforce. Forced by the isolated position of Quarry Bank to provide housing, they were quick to recognise what an invaluable tool of management this could be. Good housing, varied diet and, most importantly, security of employment in an age of uncertainty ensured loyalty and helped to guarantee peaceful labour relations, low labour turnover and greater efficiency.

One of the most interesting issues in a study of the development of the cotton industry was the rise and decline of the country mill. Initially the most efficient source of energy and the basis of the industrial revolution, water power was not finally overtaken by steam in the cotton industry until the 1830s. By the end of the nineteenth century water power had become a rarity, Quarry Bank being one of the survivors. The factors creating changes in energy sources in the cotton industry and the rationale behind choice of power source provide one of the continuing themes of the book.

Regularly neglected in studies of the development of Britain's premier Victorian industry has been the marketing mechanism. Samuel Greg's early career was as a merchant and he continued to develop this aspect of activities, sometimes misguidedly, after he became a millowner. Examination of this branch of the family business provides interesting insight into the complex and often fragmented organisation of markets in the industry, as well as the decision-making process and changing function of this branch of the firm.

Quarry Bank Mill remains today the only lasting monument to the Greg family's efforts. Enjoyed by thousands each year, it is now a flourishing museum of the cotton industry. Passed to the National Trust with surrounding woodland and village by Mr A. C. Greg, in 1939, its present success would no doubt have pleased, though probably bemused and astounded, its founder.

CHAPTER 1

The cotton industry in the eighteenth century

Quarry Bank Mill, in Styal, is an imposing Georgian cotton mill on the banks of the River Bollin, near Wilmslow in Cheshire, and it now houses a thriving textile museum. To understand how it came to be built and its early development, it is necessary to examine the eighteenth-century business environment and the organisation of the cotton industry in that period.

The eighteenth-century economy displayed a high degree of complexity. Industry was regionally specialised and organised under variations of the domestic system. Most commerce was conducted either on a local basis, or via specialist factors and merchants in London.

Even in the early 1720s, when Defoe made his Tour of England, manufacturing was heavily regionally specialised. He talks of towns having 'some particular trade . . . which is a kind of nostrum to them, inseparable to the place, and which fixes there by nature of the thing . . . the coal trade to Newcastle; the Leeds clothing trade . . .'[1] Similarly, the West of England concentrated upon cloth production, and East Anglia upon worsted. On the other hand, the principal producer of knives and tools was Sheffield, with iron and brass ware emanating from Birmingham. Lighter textiles, such as linen and cotton mixes on the one hand and hosiery on the other, were generally produced in the North-West and the East Midlands, respectively.[2]

It is the nascent cotton industry and its organisation which is most relevant to this study. As early as the sixteenth and seventeenth centuries, textiles were of great significance to the economy of Lancashire. These included coarse woollen cloths, confusingly called Manchester cottons, as well as fustians and linens.[3] The products of Lancashire were in part consumed on the home market, though the woollens were increasingly shipped to Spain, Portugal and France. Cotton for many years coexisted with woollens, linens and small wares.[4]

By the end of the seventeenth century the output of woollens was shrinking and cotton, introduced in the sixteenth century, was being employed in three branches of the Lancashire textile trade.[5] Fustians and heavy stuffs included cotton mixed either with linen or worsted yarn, it was used with linen in bed ticking, bolstering and checks and also in smallware production. By 1750 some pure cotton cloths such as velvets and velveteens were being produced. The regional specialisation displayed in England as a whole, in the eighteenth century, was extended to Lancashire. Within the county, the South-East – together with North-East Cheshire – concentrated on linen, linen-cotton and smallware. Fustians were made around Bolton and Blackburn and linen was found throughout the rest of the county.[6]

As regional specialisation progressed and the importance of the lighter textiles grew, Manchester became the major commercial centre, especially for South-East Lancashire, where it was: 'the very London of those parts, the liver that sends blood into all the counties thereabouts'.[7] Soon this influence spread over the whole county, the growing output of the country manufacturers passing through the hands of Manchester merchants.

Textile manufacturing, like most of England's industrial production, was organised under the domestic system in the eighteenth century. The low value of the raw materials, the cheapness and simplicity of hand spinning wheels, cards and looms and the ease with which processes could be subdivided made it ideal for this mode of production.[8] In Lancashire, by the eighteenth century, there were as elsewhere in the country some variations in the form of organisation. Increasingly, the large merchant-manufacturers who, like the West of England clothiers, 'scattered life and its supports to everyone around' predominated, though there were still a few independent weavers.[9] Employers of outworkers fell into two broad categories, the country manufacturers and the Manchester merchant manufacturers. According to Guest, in 1750, the fustian masters generally

resided in the country and employed neighbouring weavers and the mode of conducting manufacture at that time was as follows:– The master gave out a warp and raw cotton to the weaver, and received them back in cloth, paying the weaver for weaving and spinning; the weaver, if the spinning was not done by his own family paid the spinner for the spinning and the spinner paid the carder and the rover . . .[10]

The master then took the pieces of cloth to Manchester and sold them to merchants who arranged for them to be finished and sold them on the home market and, increasingly, overseas.

Although some merchants continued to concentrate on commerce, many of them were also employers. As early as the seventeenth century, Humphrey Chetham of Manchester was not just a substantial merchant, he also employed people in Manchester, Ashton, Hollinwood and Eccles.[11] By the eighteenth century, as Radcliffe pointed out 'the great merchants were manufacturers, with scarcely an exception'.[12] These Manchester employers were often wealthy men,[13] employing operatives over a wide area. Many workers in rural areas combined their industrial activities with agricultural labour.

There were certain inherent problems with the 'putting out' system. These included embezzlement of raw materials, lack of quality control and irregularity of work, especially at harvest time, for many workers continued to be closely tied to agriculture. Nevertheless, when technology was static and labour fairly cheap, it was possible to expand output effectively, without any change in organisation.

Because of the prevalence of the putting out system, there existed a network of middlemen who were agents for both the merchants and manufacturers. For example, both the country manufacturers and the Manchester merchant/employers sometimes used agents for the distribution of raw materials, the collection of finished goods and the payment of wages. This subcontracting by employers significantly reduced the time they spent travelling around the country districts, though it did of course increase costs.

Middlemen were not just important to manufacturing. A growing number had emerged in distribution. In a period of limited and slow communications, such agents were essential if manufacturers were to have access to and to react to patterns of demand. In the home trade, the fairs which had for centuries been the major centres of distribution began to decline in importance in the eighteenth century. Instead a growing 'number of riders . . . [took] orders for all kinds of merchandise . . .'[14] In addition, many Manchester merchants had links with London factors and warehousemen who were in close contact with the tastes and preferences of the metropolis. Similarly, it was these London agents and, by the eighteenth century, their Liverpool counterparts who co-ordinated foreign trade in Lancashire products.[15] Imported raw materials, such as cotton and flax, were increasingly dealt with by Liverpool brokers although, until the middle of the eighteenth century, London was the largest importer of raw cotton.[16]

Not only was there a network of middlemen in the eighteenth century, but commerce was bound together by a complex system of credit. As Defoe asserted, credit was 'the choicest jewel the tradesman is trusted with . . . [since] if a man has £10,000 in money he may certainly trade for £10,000 and if he has no credit he cannot trade for a shilling more'.[17] Raw materials were purchased and goods sold on credit; the main instrument was the bill of exchange, which was often drawn on a London factor. Credit terms varied, though it was customary to buy on long credit and sell on short. Thus J. and N. Philips, the Manchester smallware producers, usually bought yarn at twelve months' credit, but only allowed their customers six months to pay.[18] In this way they ensured that they could pay their operatives and cater for other contingencies, at the same time as expanding their business.

There were, of course, hazards to this system, given the complex web of credit which developed. In rising markets, some businessmen relied too heavily on credit. A sudden fall in prices could render them unable to meet their debts. Their default could have dire consequences for the entire business community. Shock waves would be felt not just in Lancashire, but in London as well and the subsequent tightening of credit could lead to the bankruptcy of many marginal firms.

Country banks did not develop in Lancashire until late in the eighteenth century. Thus, the credit system was largely informal. Ability to gain credit was based upon individual trust and accumulated creditworthiness. Business in Lancashire was dominated by the Nonconformist community.[19] Frequent intermarriage created a 'charmed circle' of commercial families, between whom funds and short-term credit flowed freely, reinforcing members' positions. New entrants to the business world, from outside this community, inevitably found it more difficult to gain credit and customers.[20] At the same time, their ability to withstand a credit crisis was predictably low.

The Lancashire economy of the early eighteenth century was thus a complex web of commerce and manufacturing, middlemen and credit. By 1750, however, the seeds of change were being sown and the demise of the domestic system, first in spinning and much later in weaving, was the result. Several interrelated factors explain the changes which took place in the organisation of cotton spinning and the eventual development of the factory system. Of these the most important was the ending of technical inertia in the industry in the 1730s, with the invention of the flying shuttle and the hosiery frame. Moreover, the demand for cotton mixes, as a substitute for more traditional cloths, was growing. This put pressure on the domestic system of organisation and highlighted the managerial problems, especially the absence of quality control and irregularity of work inherent in it.[21]

Although intially slow to diffuse, the flying shuttle and the hosiery frame were beginning to create supply bottlenecks in spinning by

1760, as the output of weavers and framework knitters increased.[22] At first, of course, it was possible for manufacturers to employ more spinners, which meant putting out materials over a wider area. This, however, not only increased transport costs but also the number of middlemen to co-ordinate operations.[23] Faced with eroded profit margins, employers were eager to reduce costs. At the same time, the irregularity of work at harvest time and inadequate quality control were growing problems as demand grew.

The bottlenecks in the spinning sector were solved by technical and organisational changes. The invention, first of the Jenny by Hargreaves in 1764 and then Arkwright's roller frames in 1769, substantially increased production of coarser yarns. Crompton's mule of 1779 allowed finer threads to be spun mechanically. The inventions themselves did not, however, make the demise of the domestic system in spinning inevitable. Early Jennies had only eight spindles, whilst the roller frame could be operated by hand. Although these machines were beyond the means of the average cottager, employers could have rented them out. The desire for greater supervision of workers led employers to build workshops, for both weaving and spinning, where operations could be closely monitored. Arkwright, however, recognised the potential of powered machinery for the expansion of output. He applied horse power and then water power to his spinning machines at Cromford and achieved a combination of sharply rising output and close supervision.[24] Inevitably, other manufacturers followed suit, attracted by Arkwright's high profit margins. Although initially the operation of his patents restricted diffusion, these lapsed in the mid-1780s. By 1787 there were said to be 143 Arkwright-type factories. By 1795 Chapman has estimated there were 300.[25] These water-powered mills were in rural areas 'where streams were found, capable of affording the requisite power to work the machinery ... In the neighbourhood of many, indeed most of these new erections, the population was extremely limited ... '[26] As a result, most early cotton masters imported labour. This was often from parish poorhouses, though some masters offered houses, gardens and even livestock to attract workers.[27]

The domestic system in cotton spinning, therefore, gave way to factory production. At the same time, the new machines ensured that pure cotton cloth could be produced cheaply and easily. Given the changes in demand for yarn, such a shift was the most rational move for employers. It is true that, initially, the existence of a surplus of under-employed agricultural labour allowed for expansion of output, without substantial rises in labour costs. It has been shown, however, that other costs did rise. It has been suggested that a firm's organisation will ultimately restrict its growth. This is because, in the absence of change in structure, costs will ultimately begin to rise as output grows. This arises from increasing inefficiency of an inappropriate form of organisation[28] and is exactly what happened in cotton spinning. Just as, in a later age, the private family partnership gave way to the joint stock company so, in the eighteenth century, the domestic system gave way to the factory.

The shift towards the factory system thus involved more than just the adoption of new technology; it meant a whole new method of organisation. The movement was, however, fairly gradual and, for many years, only involved the spinning and preparatory processes; weaving remained predominantly under the domestic system until the 1820s. The factory system involved some changes in methods of management and the nature of capital, but it was the result of a gradual evolution, rather than a radical transformation.[29] Therefore, although the movement of production into the factory did represent a change in organisation, methods of finance remained dominated by the family. Similarly, whilst the relationship between employer and employed was much closer than under the putting out system, methods of labour management were broadly traditional. The subcontract and the payment of wages on piece rates or, in some cases, in 'truck' were all survivors of the pre-industrial period.[30] Even labour recruitment which, when cotton mills relied on water power involved the importation of workers, often used traditional sources. Of these, one of the most popular in the early days at least was the parish poorhouse. Parish apprentices had been available to employers from the seventeenth century and had been extensively used under the domestic system throughout the country.[31] The provision of housing by employers was not such a radical departure as it first appears. Landowners had long provided housing for their workers and their paternalistic attitude to their labourers was imitated by the factory colonisers.[32]

The changes in the organisation of the cotton industry were gradually introduced by a group of businessmen who recognised not only the potential profitability of new types of cloth but also the improved efficiency of new methods of production. The very personal nature of finance during the industrial revolution meant that business success was inextricably tied to the fortunes of an entrepreneur's family. As Mathias pointed out 'the first rule for the successful entrepreneur was to choose his parents wisely – or at least the rest of his family'.[33] Funds for investment, partners and experience all came from within the family circle. Mathias could have added that if the prospective mill-owner's family was already established in commerce and industry and, better still, if they were Nonconformist, then his chances of success were greatly enhanced. Although by no means all early cotton millowners came from the mercantile groups, a very high proportion did;[34] Chapman has shown that 28 per cent of the cotton spinning firms set up in the North of England during the early years of the industrial revolution were headed by Manchester fustian merchants.[35] This is hardly surprising, given the rise of both Manchester and the fustian branch of Lancashire's industry during the eighteenth century. Moreover, the merchants and more especially the merchant/employers were in a strong position to appreciate changing market trends and, consequently, the potential of the cotton industry for development. The disproportionate number of Nonconformists who became factory owners has given rise to debate among historians, sociologists and even psychologists. They have variously concluded that it was the 'protestant work ethic', the superior education or the need for achievement of Nonconformists which led them to become pioneer industrialists in the late eighteenth century.[36] Lively though the debate has been, such conclusions remain unconvincing. Instead, Peter Payne's suspicion that 'the over representation of non-conformists among the entrepreneurs who attained prominence . . . [was] . . . because they belonged to extended kinship families . . . [which] . . . gave them access to credit . . . '[37] seems more plausible. Additionally, since the business community was already dominated by Non-conformists, it was only to be expected that millowners would reflect this bias.

Change in the eighteenth-century industry thus largely came from within. The wealth created under the domestic system was trans-mitted, often via kinship links, into factories. The goodwill created by earlier generations made credit readily available to some factory masters. Thus, the business environment of the eighteenth century was far from being the perfectly competitive world which is sometimes imagined. It is true that there were none of the large firms associated with today's corporate economy. By modern standards, there was a very low level of concentration of business in the hands of individual firms, with firms tending to be small. However, because of inter-marriage, religious and other links within the business community, regional economies were often more dominated by a few family groups than is immediately apparent. This is not to say that there were no newcomers, but that their lack of connections and consequent limited access to credit and markets may have restricted the growth of their firms and made them more likely to fail.

Samuel Greg, who founded Quarry Bank mill in 1784, came from a long-established mercantile family. In a world where inherited wealth and connections counted for much, this allowed him to make the most of the opportunities with which he was presented.

CHAPTER 2

Samuel Greg and Quarry Bank Mill, 1783–1815

Samuel Greg pursued a successful business career at Manchester and Quarry Bank, throughout the turbulent Napoleonic War period. A fustian merchant by training, Greg, like many of his contemporaries in Manchester, moved into factory spinning during the 1780s. Using water power from the River Bollin and a high proportion of pauper labour, Greg developed his cotton mill at Styal. A combination of inheritance, business shrewdness and a fair measure of luck enabled him to survive the difficult war period and laid the foundation for expansion during the 1820s. He started his career with a generous inheritance of £36,000. During the war period, despite some mistakes, his investment policy was basically sound and he amassed a fortune of £230,000 from which he built up one of the giants of the cotton industry. His firm, by 1834, consisted of five spinning and weaving mills, employing upwards of 2,000 people. These were served by a sales division which also sold the products of other firms.

I Samuel Greg's background

Samuel Greg was born in Belfast in 1758, the second surviving son of Thomas and Elizabeth Greg. Thomas had married Elizabeth Hyde in 1742,[1] and the couple had thirteen children. It was a typical union of two commercial families. Thomas Greg was a substantial merchant and shipowner at the time of his marriage. Samuel Hyde, Elizabeth's father, was a small Lancashire landowner who became involved in the Belfast linen trade, though how this came about is unclear. It was the Hydes who provided one of the major keys to Samuel Greg's later business success. Thomas Greg became a wealthy man. By 1785 he had business ventures in America, Russia and England, as well as Ireland, and he owned land in both North America and the West Indies.[2] He experienced frequent financial difficulties as a result of

13

Thomas Greg and family: Samuel extreme right

speculating in trade and later in minerals. This, combined with the liability of an ever growing family, meant that when his childless brother-in-law, Robert Hyde, offered to adopt and educate the eight-year-old Samuel, in 1766, he had no qualms about letting the boy go. Robert and his brother Nathaniel had expanded their father's linen business and it must have seemed an excellent opportunity. From then on Thomas had little contact with his son and his will, in which he left Samuel only £300 and a parcel of land worth around £500 in New York State, suggests he felt his son was already provided for.[3]

Samuel completed his formal education at school in Harrow (not *the* Harrow School), in 1778. His uncle, Robert, was keen for him to join the family business but Nathaniel, jealous of his nephew, urged that he should become a minister. He was overruled and Samuel joined the firm.[4] In 1750, Robert Hyde had set about expanding his father's firm. He set up a merchant-manufacturing partnership in Manchester with Robert Hamilton.[5] The partnership flourished and, by its dissolution in 1762, had trade debts of £20,000 in its favour.[6] Linen yarns from the Hydes' Belfast firm were put out to Lancashire cottagers and woven into fustians and other coarse cloths. These were then sold in the home market, in Ireland and America. After Robert Hamilton's retirement, Nathaniel Hyde joined his brother and, together, they expanded the scope of their firm. By 1782, Hyde and Company of Chancery Lane was one of Manchester's largest merchant-manufac-turers. They continued to sell their own produce at home and abroad but also become yarn and cloth dealers. Additionally, as commission agents, they acted on behalf of other putters out.[7]

Samuel Greg owed his career to his uncles. They provided him with an invaluable business training and considerable wealth and, perhaps most important, the wide range of trading connections, which accom-panies long establishment. As a young man of twenty, Samuel Greg began learning as much as possible about the textile trade and 'travelled the continent taking orders for the House of Hyde and [became] a regular manufacturer in Manchester of stuffs, chiefly velveteens, nankeens and quiltings'.[8] He enjoyed travelling, though he was irritated by the haggling of the Italians, who were one of his principal customers.[9] In 1780, his apprenticeship served, he became a junior partner in the firm. It was not long before he became a very wealthy man. In 1782, Robert Hyde died, leaving him £10,000. This was not all, however, for by this time Nathaniel Hyde was a confirmed alcoholic and had to retire. This meant that Samuel took over the firm. Stocks of cloth were valued at £26,691, mainly held in fustians.[10] Samuel Greg, in partnership with John Middleton, took possession of this stock and paid Nathaniel 5 per cent per annum interest over a five-year period. Additionally, a financial reserve of not more than £10,000 was put at their disposal.[11] The ending of the American War of Independence provided an unanticipated bonus: it increased the value of stocks by £13,000. All this meant that Greg was in an exceptional financial position, just when extraordinary investment opportunities were opening up. Beyond this, the goodwill of the House of Hyde gave him customers and access to credit. In addition, since the Hydes were amongst the leaders of Manchester's Non-conformist society, he also gained business connections of the first quality. Manchester, although comparatively small at the end of the eighteenth century, was a growing town. A commercial rather than industrial centre, it remained sufficiently attractive for many merchants to live there. They met on a daily basis through business and pleasure. In a world where personal contact was the essence of success, this was most important. From the start Greg was closely acquainted with such influential commercial families as the Philipses, Hibberts and Heywoods,[12] and became part of the Nonconformist commercial network. By joining the Manchester Literary and Philosophical Society in 1790, a body dominated by Nonconformist businessmen, he further consolidated his position.[13] A newcomer would have taken years to acquire such a situation.

Well established in business, Samuel thus moved easily in Manchester society and also had connections in Liverpool, the home of his bride. He was 29 when he married Hannah Lightbody, the third daughter of Adam Lightbody, a Unitarian merchant from Liverpool. She was a highly intelligent woman, whose liberal and humanitarian outlook on life came from her upbringing. Throughout their long marriage, she gave Samuel sympathy and understanding – no easy task when, as an old man, he became increasingly stubborn. There were frequent clashes of temperament, especially between Samuel and his second son, Robert. Hannah did not always agree with her husband, but acted as peacemaker.[14] Quarry Bank House, their home from 1796, was noted for its cultured atmosphere, and this must have been a welcome change from the rigours of business life.[15] Visitors were impressed with its simplicity and the family's obvious contentment. One visitor commented '. . . have you ever been to Quarry Bank? It is such a picture of rational happy life. Mr Greg is quite a gentleman, his daughters have the delightful simplicity of people perfectly satisfied in their place and never trying to get out of it.'[16] Another recalled 'We stayed a week with them and admired the cultivation of mind and refinement of manners which Mrs Greg

Hannah Greg

preserved in the midst of money making and the somewhat un-
polished community of merchants and manufacturers. Mr Greg too
was most gentlemanly and hospitable and [was] surrounded by
clever, well conducted children.'[17]

Samuel's marriage to Hannah benefited his business. Not only did
she bring him a dowry of £10,000,[18] but her family connections proved
to be extremely important. Hannah's sisters, Elizabeth and Agnes,
married into textile families. Elizabeth married Thomas Hodgson, a
Liverpool merchant in the African trade, with cotton mills at Caton,
near Lancaster.[19] Agnes married Thomas Pares of the Leicestershire
banking family, which also had textile interests in Derbyshire. (see
Figure 2.1). Both these connections proved useful later on. It was from
the Hodgsons, in payment of a business debt, that Greg acquired a
small cotton mill at Caton, near Lancaster,[20] while both families
supplied him with loans. Samuel Greg, therefore, had a very sound
basis upon which to build his business. He had inherited a thriving
textile firm. This, combined with extensive family links and a degree of

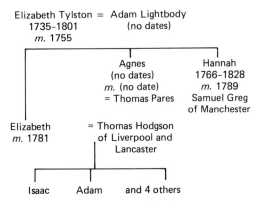

Figure 2.1 The Lightbody family tree

business acumen, enabled him not only to become a cotton millowner but, later, to head a vast business empire.

II Quarry Bank, 1784–1815

It has been shown that it was a logical step for established merchant-manufacturers to become millowners.[21] In the early 1780s, the Hydes had already moved towards becoming factory owners by building a hand weaving shed at Eyam, in Derbyshire. In this way they could better control the quality of cloth produced while, at the same time, guaranteeing steady production. By 1783, however, it was clear to Samuel that a regular supply of yarn was essential, if output at Eyam was to progress smoothly. For this reason work began on Quarry Bank Mill at Styal in 1783.[22]

Why Samuel should have chosen a site in Cheshire, many miles from his Eyam shed, remains a mystery. It is true that the water site on the River Bollin, near Wilmslow, proved to be an unusually good one. It seems unlikely, however, that in 1783 Samuel was aware of its potential. One possibility is that Arkwright's activities in Derbyshire meant that prime sites in the county were becoming scarce and, because of rising water rights, expensive. Whatever the explanation, Greg chose the deep, wooded valley of the Bollin, near Styal, to build his first cotton mill.

That he waited until 1783 before starting work is interesting. It was the year that the American War of Independence ended. This potentially widened the market for cotton goods – as the rise in the value of his stocks suggests. As a result, many manufacturers began to expand production, and a wave of investment, which lasted until 1787, began.[23] Equally significant was the ongoing controversy surrounding Arkwright's patents. Until 1781 Arkwright had, via his patents for cotton spinning and carding, restricted the use of his devices by licence. The latter were expensive and there were many infringements. Ultimately, his patent rights were challenged by manufacturers who objected to his powerful position. A series of lawsuits followed. In 1781 his carding patent was declared invalid whilst, in 1783, the spinning patent was due to expire. Thus, many manufacturers, including Samuel Greg, were encouraged to build cotton mills free from the burden of Arkwright's licence fee. In 1785, Arkwright was able to overthrow the earlier verdict, but his success was short-lived. In November of that year his patent was finally cancelled.[24] This was, no doubt, much to the relief of the new millowners who, like Samuel Greg, would have otherwise faced heavy licence fees.

Although Samuel Greg had wealth, experience and business connections, he was essentially a merchant and lacked technical expertise – a common problem at the time. His aim, in the early years, was to continue in this capacity using the mill to supply his hand-loom weavers, rather than being directly involved in its operation. Nevertheless, he was keen that it should run smoothly and efficiently. Thus, whilst supplying the necessary capital to build the small mill, he took a partner, John Massey. Nothing is known about Massey's background. It is, however, likely that, as was common at the time, Greg advertised in the Manchester newspapers for a technically competent partner to superintend the building and equipping of the mill. It was also intended that Massey should run the mill whilst Greg remained in Manchester. Unfortunately, in 1784, he died just before Quarry Bank Mill started operations.[25] This placed Greg in a quandary, for he now had a mill and no one to run it. He lacked both the time and inclination to do this himself because his mercantile business needed his attention. His solution was to rely on his manager, Matthew Fawkner, about whose backbround nothing is known, to run the mill. This arrangement lasted for the next 12 years. During this time Greg's main interests were commercial.[26] He visited Quarry Bank regularly, but did not move from Manchester to live permanently at Styal until 1796. It is probable that his reluctance to leave his home at No. 35 King Street was due, in part, to a fear that distance from the nucleus of trade and the absence of daily contact with other merchants would damage his business. At first it seems strange – and certainly in this period unusual – for Greg to have relied on his manager to run his mill.

Investment in buildings and machinery is far more risky than operating under the putting out system. This is because fixed assets are not
readily realisable in times of crisis or slump. Nor by the standards of
the time was Quarry Bank especially small; it was a typical Arkwright-
type mill which cost around £3,000 to build and equip.[27] In compari-
son with the value of his turnover in Manchester or his inheritance,
however, this sum was paltry. It could almost be seen as an experiment, the responsibility for which he was happy to delegate to his
manager.

Very little is known about Greg's first 12 years at Quarry Bank.
About 150 operatives were initially employed to spin coarse yarn on
water frames.[28] In those early days Greg '... had to use any cotton
which could be got or worked on current machinery, Bourbon, West
Indian and Brazilian ...'[29] It is likely that he also experimented with
American cotton, since his suppliers, the Rathbones, made the first
known importation in 1784. It was not, however, until 1808 that
America became his major source of supply.[30] Development was slow
in this period and apart from the replacement of the water wheel in
1792[31] and the provision of cottages, some of which were converted
farm buildings, and an Apprentice House for his imported workforce
in 1790,[32] there was little new expenditure at Styal before 1796, when
spindlage stood at 2,425.[33] This suggests there was a water wheel of
about 20 horse power. Greg obviously had sufficient funds to have
expanded Quarry Bank between 1784 and 1796 had he wished. It is
true that the isolated position of the mill meant that labour had to be
brought to Styal, but there is nothing to suggest that shortage of
workers was responsible for slow growth; parish poorhouses proved a
very fruitful source of labour.[34]

The reasons for the slow growth must remain speculative, since data
are inadequate. However, production at Quarry Bank remained
closely linked to that at Eyam[35] and to the condition of the home cloth
market. This was because at this time yarn exports were frowned upon
as the cause of potential foreign competition.[36] The numerous crises
and slumps – the product of some over-capacity and growing
uncertainty about the prospects of war – provided little inducement
for expansion.[37] In any event, Greg's lack of technical expertise was an
obstacle to growth, since it prevented him from harnessing additional
power from the Bollin. For whatever reason, Greg showed little
inclination to invest further in his cotton mill, his relative lack of
interest being shown by his continued residence in Manchester.

Ironically, it was probably the advent of war with France, in 1793,
which accelerated the growth of the firm. It is true that the war

Front of mill, showing old mill 1784–96 and part of new mill

increased risk and closed some markets, but it also created opportunities. The commercial end of the business expanded, sometimes with dangerous consequences. On the production side, scale increased but, of even greater importance, its direction changed fundamentally. From concentrating on the production of cloth, Greg moved towards yarn production, exclusively. Eyam was run down and abandoned around 1807,[38] though it is likely that some hand-weaving continued at Styal. Quarry Bank, on the other hand, from being a satellite of Eyam, became a highly profitable production unit, specialising in coarse yarns. Recognising the danger of over-specialisation in wartime, Greg experimented with finer, mule-spun yarns at Styal until 1806. This was successful, but it was difficult to expand in a country area, where skilled labour was hard to come by. He therefore abandoned this at Quarry Bank and built a mule mill in Peter Street, Manchester, in 1807.[39]

At what point Greg decided to abandon Eyam and concentrate on spinning is unclear. It may be that in expanding Quarry Bank in the late 1790s, he was intending to increase cloth output. He was, after all, in a strong position to exploit American markets, having a range of contacts there. His uncles had traded with Philadelphia, earlier in the century. Moreover, in the early 1790s, his brother-in-law, James Lyle, who had some experience in the Atlantic trade, became his commercial partner.[40] The capacity of the firm to sell cloth in the former colonies (not just of their own production), may have encouraged Greg to expand his own cloth output. If such was the case, the heavy debts incurred in the trade in the early 1800s may have persuaded Greg that such expansion was imprudent, leading him to change direction. Alternatively, it is possible that he always intended to phase out the hand-weaving shed, and that the delay resulted from the time it took to increase spinning capacity at Styal and experiment with fine yarn production. The first explanation is the most plausible. Many cloth producers and exporters suffered in the early years of the nineteenth century. Previously taboo yarn exports were, on the other hand, growing, which led to high prices in 1805.[41] This possibly encouraged Greg to transfer his entire operations to spinning and expand Quarry Bank.

Without further technical help, however, Greg would have been unable to take advantage of these opportunities. Archaeological evidence, on site at Styal, suggests that his original use of power was most inefficient and incapable of supporting any additional production.[42] He was, therefore, fortunate in persuading Peter Ewart to

Samuel Greg as a young man

join him in partnership in 1796. Peter Ewart was a highly competent engineer, with the '. . . singular advantage of being formed in the best school of practical mechanics and engineering . . .',[43] having trained with Boulton and Watt. On completing his training Ewart became a traveller for the firm, selling steam engines and gaining an intimate knowledge of power systems for cotton mills. It is likely that it was on a visit to the North-West that he first met Samuel Greg.

The terms of the partnership were apparently generous, so keen was Greg to gain Ewart's expertise. Ewart, therefore, contributed a mere £400 capital, yet enjoyed a quarter of spinning profits and a sixth of marketing. At Quarry Bank, however, the spinning partnership was to pay Samuel Greg an annual rent on expenditure on building

The weir

and machinery. That the figure on which this was calculated was nearly four times the insured value of the mill and that Ewart agreed to it, suggests that he felt the site had considerable potential.[44]

Work began almost immediately and by 1801 a dam and a stone weir to conserve and control the water were completed and two new water wheels installed.[45] In 1807 a further new water wheel, with a tunnel to take off the headwater, was added, followed in 1810 by a 10-horse-power Boulton and Watt steam engine to provide supplementary power.[46] As a result the labour force grew, more parish apprentices were taken and new families came to Styal. The village, therefore, became larger and eight new cottages were built. The cost of this expansion was £8,622, with a further £800 being spent on the new dwellings.[47] Table 2.1 shows that productive capacity at Quarry Bank was substantially increased as a result of this expenditure and that by the end of the Napoleonic Wars, the mill had become fairly large by the standards of the time. Expansion was not, however, confined to Quarry Bank. Work began on a mule-spinning mill in Peter Street, Manchester in 1807. The mill, which by 1811 had 12,400 spindles, cost £23,981 to build and equip.[48] Both concerns were very successful, with returns running high. At Quarry Bank these averaged 18 per cent a

Table 2.1 *The development of Quarry Bank, 1790–1816*

	Spindlage	Numbers employed	Power Water (hp)	Steam (hp)	Yarn output (lb)	Share of total yarn market (%)
1790	n.a.	205	n.a.	—	n.a.	n.a.
1796	2,425	n.a.	*c.* 20	—	n.a.	n.a.
1805	3,356	n.a.	n.a.	—	213,616	n.a.
1815–16	4,416	252	*c.* 40	10	342,578	0.4

Sources: MCL C5/3/2/2, Samuel Greg's personal account; MCL C5/1/15/1, Quarry Bank wages book; S. D. Chapman, *The early factory masters* (Newton Abbot 1967), p. 128; *Report on the state of children . . .*, PP 1816 (397) III, p. 374; T. Ellison, *The cotton trade of Great Britain* (new impression 1968, first published 1886), p. 56.

year between 1802 and 1811, whilst in Manchester profits averaged £3,846 a year between 1808 and 1814.[49]

High profits, however, were a reflection of the high levels of risk faced by manufacturers and merchants during the Napoleonic Wars. In a period of extreme uncertainty, profits could all too easily be replaced by vast losses, as Greg found in his mercantile firm, when losses totalling £31,864 were incurred in Spain at the end of the war.[50] To a less established or substantial businessman such losses could have been catastrophic; to Greg they were serious but not fatal. He tried to safeguard his position by diversifying his investment, as Table 2.2 shows. Thus, although he retained 60 per cent of his assets in the cotton industry, (largely in liquid assets), he invested in land and other outlets. With rents high, land represented a safe and remunerative investment during the war period. It is not surprising, therefore, that Greg purchased the small Oak Estate, Styal, from the Earl of Stamford in 1802, and some land in Reddish, near Stockport in Cheshire, in 1804. This formed part of what was to become Greg's Reddish Estate, a property which was valued at £30,000 in 1814. These estates, combined with land in the West Indies (inherited from his father and his uncle), and those in New York State, provided an excellent insurance against trade reverses. His one mistake in this sphere lay in the purchase of some land near the centre of Manchester at the end of the eighteenth century, as a speculation on the town's expansion. When this slowed down, he was left for many years unable to sell or to develop it.[51]

Table 2.2 *Samuel Greg's assets, 1814*

Type of investment	%
Cotton industry	63.9
Land	24.8
Public utilities	1.0
Government stock	4.4
Miscellaneous	5.9

Source: MCL C5/1/1, Samuel Greg's assets, reprinted from M. B. Rose, 'The role of the family as providers of capital and managerial talent in Samuel Greg and Company, 1784–1840', *BH*19 (1977), p. 50 (with consent of *BH*).

In the 31 years after Samuel Greg founded Quarry Bank he not only survived a period of extreme trade uncertainty, but emerged from the war in an exceptionally strong position to enjoy whatever post-war prosperity there might be. Notwithstanding losses in Spain at the end of the war, he amassed a considerable fortune. In 1782 his assets, including stocks of goods, totalled slightly more than £36,000. By 1814 these had increased to £230,711, which, even allowing for wartime inflation, was a substantial rise.[52] It is hard to establish how far this fortune was created by fortuitous circumstances and how far by Greg's business acumen. What is certain is that his path was eased by his original inheritance, both of funds and contacts. These enabled him to respond to market changes, as they arose, whilst creating opportunities where none had previously existed.

III Labour supply

It is generally agreed that the availability of an abundant supply of cheap labour is of fundamental importance to British industrialisation.[53] Its existence was principally the result of population growth. Between 1701 and 1771 population grew steadily, at an average rate of 0.39 per cent per annum. From 1780, however, it surged forward, and between 1781 and 1800 grew at a rate of 0.91 per cent per annum.[54] Growth continued and between 1801 and 1851 the population of Great Britain almost doubled, to stand at 20.9 million.[55] Population growth on its own did not create a labour force. Obstacles to mobility, combined with the need to locate early factories in rural areas close to water supplies, meant that many early millowners like Samuel Greg needed to import labour. Children were especially sought after and, until legislation rendered it uneconomic in the 1830s, child labour was extensively used in cotton mills. Millowners were keen to create an efficient workforce, prepared to work regular hours. The establishment of a factory labour force during the industrial revolution thus involved not only importation of workers to isolated areas but the training and disciplining of such a workforce to mill work.

The provision of housing close to rural mills could fulfil the dual function of inducing families to move to the area and of controlling them, once they were there. The strong prejudice against mill work in the eighteenth century meant that even the prospect of a cheap and relatively comfortable house was insufficient to persuade many workers to move voluntarily. Moreover, the operation of the Settlement Laws may have discouraged movement. The growing number of paupers, especially in London, meant that whilst it may have been difficult to attract 'free' operatives, millowners had a ready pool of labour from which to draw. Parish poorhouses, whether as a source of indentured labour or of parish apprentices, were invaluable during the early phases of the industrial revolution. They meant that water power could be used extensively *despite* the isolated position of many mills.

Like his contemporaries elsewhere, Samuel Greg was attracted to Styal by the water supply, not by the number of potential operatives in the area. Quarry Bank could not have been developed without imported labour. The tiny hamlet supported only a scattered community of farmers and agricultural workers. Even if the nearby village of Morley is included, the indigenous population was sparse. Communications were poor in the 1780s and rural communities were largely static. Thus not only was Styal, a mere 11 miles from Manchester, geographically isolated, but few if any of its inhabitants were likely to have known anything about cotton mills. As a result, even if there had been enough villagers to staff Quarry Bank in 1784, they almost certainly viewed Greg – the first cotton master in the area – with distrust. They were used to working in their cottages, combining any domestic industry with agriculture. The idea of working regular hours, herded together under one roof, was alien to them. There was not even much of a textile tradition in the area. A few cottagers did some jersey spinning, but most finished mohair buttons, put out by Macclesfield manufacturers.[56] Even the prospect of higher wages than they could earn in agriculture was unlikely to be much of a temptation. In a modern society geared to consumption, it is easy to forget that, in the eighteenth century, there was very little incentive to increase earnings. This is because there was so little on which to spend wages, especially in rural areas and regular saving was unheard of, amongst all but the wealthy.

Greg, however, can have had few worries about finding operatives for his mill. During the late eighteenth century parish poorhouses were keen to dispatch as many inmates as possible into whatever employment presented itself. This, no doubt, encouraged him to build his mill in such an isolated district. That he had few difficulties recruiting his workforce is confirmed by the size of Quarry Bank. Up to 1841 most mills in Lancashire employed fewer than 200 workers, yet by 1816 there were 252 operatives at Quarry Bank.[57]

Where the hard core of Greg's initial workforce came from is unclear. He may have brought some experienced spinners from the Eyam area or elsewhere in Derbyshire (the early centre of factory-based cotton spinning), possibly even poaching from established millowners like Arkwright and Strutt. Requirements for the new mill were limited anyway, and it was probably some years before Quarry Bank was working at full capacity. What is apparent, however, is that Greg was in no hurry to create a permanent community at Styal, preferring instead to import numerous children from parish poor-houses. Until the 1840s more than half the workforce was children. This in part explains his attachment to parish children – he perceived that it was cheaper to build an apprentice house for 90 children at a cost of £300 and support them in it than to build cottages, costing between £50 and £100, for whole families,[58] especially when there were few jobs for adults. It is, of course, also possible that the very availability of these children in large numbers may have encouraged his policies.

Styal village thus grew very slowly. Initially, Greg started by converting some farm buildings into dwellings during the 1780s. The cottages in Shaw's Fold, for example, are converted outhouses, whilst part of Farm Fold was, originally, a Dutch Barn. Although he did begin building in 1790, only 16 cottages were built in the next 30 years. This policy changed in the 1820s, when he undertook a dramatic expansion of his mill.

The parish apprenticeship system was widely used by cotton manufacturers. It was the binding of poor children into trades for a period of around seven years. It was envisaged that, during this time, they would learn a trade by which they could support themselves in later life. Such was the original intention when the system was formalised in the Elizabethan Poor Law.[59] By the late eighteenth century conditions and attitudes had changed. Between 1776 and 1785

Farm Fold Cottages, showing Dutch barn structure

expenditure on poor relief rose from £1,529,980 per annum to £2,004,238 per annum.[60] From being concerned that children should be trained, overseers, especially those in London, were increasingly looking for ways of reducing their commitments. It was demonstrably cheaper to apprentice poor children (even though the parish had to pay the premium) than to support them in the poorhouse, so it became more and more popular. Extension of the Settlement Laws to include apprenticeship in 1691 meant that if a binding was in another parish, that parish paid any future poor relief. As a result, hard-pressed overseers had the incentive '. . . to bind out poor children apprentices no matter to whom or to what trade, but to take especial care the master live in another parish . . .'[61] Thus, when rural manufacturers needed labour, it was forthcoming, sometimes in their own locality but more often from urban centres. It was not unusual in the 1770s and 1780s to find overseers advertising the availability of children in the local press or in the manufacturing areas. So it was that the Nottingham overseers proclaimed that they had 'Several healthy boys of 11 or 12 years of age ready to be apprenticed into the country',[62] whilst the overseers of the parish of Oswestry placed the following notice in

Wheeler's Manchester Chronicle: 'Manufacturers and mechanics may be supplied with either boys or girls as parish apprentices from 8 to 16 years, all healthy children, by applying to the overseers of the poor of the parish of Oswestry, Salop . . .'[63]

The apprenticeship of large numbers of poor children usually aged between 10 and 12 years of age, many miles from their families, to work long hours in cotton mills seems barbaric. Attitudes to children, and more particularly to poor children, were very different in the late eighteenth century from those of today. It was customary for numbers of children from a variety of backgrounds to work; thus the employment of pauper apprentices in the early mills was acceptable. It is impossible to estimate how many children were apprenticed by their parishes into the cotton industry, but since a high proportion of urban parishes and, indeed, rural millowners, were involved in the transfer, the numbers must have been considerable.[64]

The cotton masters received a premium of between two and four guineas for each parish child they took. Usually, the overseers also sent a new outfit of clothes with each apprentice – indeed, many employers insisted on it. Some millowners had medical officers for their apprentices; these were employed less for the welfare of the children than for the benefit of the cotton masters. Although they frequently treated children who fell ill during their term, this was not their main function. Their primary duty was to check that all paupers bound were capable of working long hours in the hot, dusty atmosphere of a cotton mill. Any who within the first six weeks were found to be unfit were returned to their parishes.[65]

As soon as the probationary period was over, the parish children became the responsibility of the employer, who then undertook to '. . . find, provide and allow unto the said apprentice meet, competent and sufficient meat, drink, apparel, lodging, washing and other things fit for an apprentice'.[66] Most built an apprentice house for their pauper children and employed a superintendent to look after them. The extent to which individual cotton masters fulfilled their obligations varied considerably.[67] Even minimal recognition of their existence meant that employers incurred some weekly expenses and inconvenience. Yet, unlike most other forms of child labour, parish children were for the first twenty years of the industrial revolution a ready available and renewable source. They were, in addition, despite maintenance costs, cheaper than the alternatives. Without them, millowners using water power would have had to pay higher wages and invest more on cottages, to attract families.

The parish children came to Styal during the 1780s. They came from the Wilmslow poorhouse and lodged with villagers. By 1790 their numbers justified the erection of an apprentice house.[68] As labour requirements at Quarry Bank increased, Greg began to take children from a growing range of parishes. These included some local ones, such as Macclesfield and Biddulph (near Congleton) and other more distant ones, such as Newcastle under Lyme, Hackney, Chelsea and Liverpool.[69] Sometimes Greg sent agents to approach different parishes, at other times parishes contacted him. For example, in 1817 Samuel Greg received a letter from the Vicar of Biddulph who was as eager to rid his parish of poor children as Greg was to receive them. He wrote:

The thought has occurred to me that some of the younger branches of the poor of this parish might be useful to you as apprentices in your factory at Quarry Bank. If you are in want of any of the above, we could readily furnish you with 10 or more at from 9 to 12 years of age of both sexes.[70]

Greg agreed to take some girls, on the condition that the parish provided them with a complete set of clothing consisting of '2 shifts, 2 pairs of stockings, 2 frocks or bedgowns, 2 aprons . . .'[71]

By 1800 up to 90 parish apprentices (about 60 girls and 30 boys) worked at Styal – about 50 per cent of the total workforce. By 1816 the proportion had fallen, though at 36 per cent of the labour force[72] they remained important. Some employers, such as David Dale at New Lanark, William Douglas at Holywell and the Peels at Bury, relied almost exclusively on parish children. Both Dale and Douglas employed 500 parish children at one time, whilst the Peels had 1,000.[73] Although this dwarfed Greg's use of the system, the impact which it had upon Quarry Bank Mill in the early years should not be under-estimated.

For a penny or two a week and their board and lodging the ninety or so children carried out a wide range of jobs in the mill. New apprentices did the menial tasks, such as sweeping floors, doffing and piecing.[74] Some older children learnt to spin and card, whilst the most able boys became highly skilled mechanics. Though by no means the only type of labour, parish apprentices eased the creation of a factory workforce at Styal significantly. They were, for many years, an invaluable supplement to the indigenous population and, later on, formed the basis of a large, stable community at Styal. The ease with which a new batch of parish apprentices could be obtained, at least in the eighteenth century, meant that many employers turned away children at the end of their terms. Greg almost certainly did, too, though several promising ex-apprentices were retained. For example, Charles Crout, an 1808 apprentice, eventually became an overlooker.

Table 2.3 *Breakdown of cost of clothing provided by Samuel Greg for Joseph Garside, 1795*

Item	£	s	d
Shoes		4	6
Stockings		1	6
Coat		4	6
Vest		2	6
Breeches		4	0
Shirts		4	2
Hat		2	6
Total cost	1	3	8

Similarly, Francis Scott, who was apprenticed in 1819, was employed for many years as a mechanic, as was James Scotson.[75] Until the 1820s those who stayed were, however, in the minority.

Pauper apprentices were not the only children brought to Styal. There were numerous children working under contract, mostly from families receiving poor relief. Agents from Quarry Bank regularly sought after poor families who might welcome the chance of work for one or more of their offspring. Some continued to live with their parents. Others, whose home was further away, either boarded in the village or may even have joined the apprentices. Children working under contract received a weekly wage of ninepence or a shilling. Joseph Garside, for example, came to Styal from Gatley, in Cheshire, in 1795. He agreed to serve Samuel Greg '. . . for the term of six years at the wage of ninepence per week for the first year and one shilling per week the remaining part of the term . . .' Since this boy came from a poor family, Greg also agreed to clothe him, as shown in Table 2.3.[76] Although many children came alone, when adult employment was available, whole families were also recruited in this way.[77] Adult male employment was, however, more often on Oak Farm, which Greg bought in 1803, or in hand-loom weaving at home than in the actual mill.

In general, therefore, although it was necessary to import workers during the early years of Quarry Bank's development, sufficient labour, mostly pauper, was readily available. At no time did Greg complain of a shortage of labour, despite his rural position. Adherence to a policy of relatively low wages throughout suggests that he had enough operatives for his requirements.[78] Greg did not, before 1815, make strenuous efforts to create a permanent community at Styal. The regular supply of parish apprentices and other pauper children discouraged such development. It was only later, in the 1820s and 1830s, when parish children were less available and when the Factory Acts discouraged the employment of juvenile labour, that Greg seriously tried to create a stable workforce.

IV Marketing

Commerce was the source of Samuel Greg's wealth; experience and connections remained an important element of his business activity throughout. Between 1784 and 1815 Samuel Greg and Company of Manchester was not simply the outlet for the produce of Greg mills. It remained an independent mercantile partnership, pursuing an adventurous and sometimes hazardous sales policy. As cloth merchants,[79] rather than agents, the firm bore the risks of overseas trade during the Napoleonic Wars. The losses which he incurred before 1815 led Greg to transform the firm in later years into one which was the servant of his mills.

When Greg inherited Hyde and Company he was in partnership with a certain John Middleton. From 1784, when Middleton withdrew, until the early 1790s, when he was joined by his brother-in-law, James Lyle and shortly afterwards by Peter Ewart, Greg ran the firm alone. Initially, he pursued similar policies to those of his uncles, selling cloth in Europe and the West Indies. He did, however, extend the breadth of his business from the 1790s onwards, forging trading links with Russia and America. The American trade was based on Philadelphia and New York and was managed by James Lyle. It was expanded when war made trade with Europe increasingly uncertain. It grew in importance, so that between 1801 and 1804, 59 per cent of the firm's cloth consignments were to America.[80]

Trading losses were heavy after 1801, averaging £780 a year between 1801 and 1808.[81] Bad debts in the American trade were exceptionally high, and over the same period averaged £24,014.[82] James Lyle, who had been responsible for arrangements in America, resigned from what he described as a 'losing concern' in 1806.[83] It could be, however, that his mismanagement of the American business, especially his failure to assess the credit-worthiness of customers was the cause of the debts. Peter Ewart also resigned from the marketing partnership in the same year – seemingly to devote himself to the Manchester mule mill – though he may have been alarmed by the poor performance of the sales firm.

For some years, sales policies became more cautious. Overseas business shrank and profitability improved. Between 1809 and 1813 Samuel Greg, in partnership with his warehouseman, Garner Daniel, earned profits averaging £3,109 a year.[84] The change of policy was doubtless in part as a result of previous losses and also because the Continental blockade and American embargoes severely restricted overseas trade after 1807.

As the war progressed, however, the effectiveness of these restrictions declined and, from 1813, Greg – in partnership with his nephew Isaac Hodgson and Garner Daniel – began expanding his foreign business again. By 1815 he was trading with Italy, France, America, Russia, Spain, Germany and South America.[85]

As before, this wartime trade proved hazardous and for a smaller, less well-established firm, it could have been fatal. Exchange rate fluctuations, combined with the changing attitudes of foreign governments, led to severe losses during the closing stages of the war. Discussing his father's problems in 1814 and 1815, Robert Hyde Greg explained 'The goods for dollars at 6 shillings each were paid for in dollars worth 4s 6d only. And goods bought when the pound was only worth 14s 6d had to be paid for at 20s 0d, the goods bought at 20s 0d fell to 14s 6d . . .'[86] The impact of these fluctuations was serious to Samuel Greg and Company, since the value of goods and debts was £124,000 in 1814.[87] At least as damaging to the firm's overseas interests was the re-entry of Ferdinand VII into Spain, also in 1814. He issued a decree that all English goods not sold within three months were to be confiscated. Despite a visit to Spain by Isaac Hodgson and Robert Hyde Greg to secure an extension, substantial losses were incurred. Indeed, the losses associated with exchange rate fluctuations and the confiscation of goods totalled £31,864. This proved ruinous to Garner Daniel, who had few assets outside the business. Isaac Hodgson met part of his debt by passing Caton Mill and the Escowbeck Estate to Samuel Greg, but Greg was forced to bear the outstanding losses himself.[88]

The difficulties encountered by Samuel Greg in marketing, between 1801 and 1815, indicate managerial deficiencies within the firm and highlight the problems and dangers of overseas trade during wartime. At first Greg was able to supervise his mercantile venture himself and delegate responsibility for his cotton mill to his manager. In 1796 he chose to move to Styal; he retained close contact with the sales firm, but decisions (especially on the American trade) were made by his brother-in-law. It is probable that as Quarry Bank grew he would have been more successful had he abandoned selling, a policy pursued by many of his contemporaries,[89] especially in overseas markets during wartime. The failures of his marketing policy illustrate the problems of a firm which has outgrown its managerial capabilities. Many of the losses incurred were the result of inadequate knowledge in highly volatile markets.

CHAPTER 3

Expansion, 1815–1834

In 1815 Samuel Greg and Company was thriving and enjoyed all the advantages of long establishment. The firm was not, however, a giant. Yet by the time of its proprietor's death, 19 years later, it had become one of the largest coarse spinning and weaving concerns in the country. During the 1820s Greg not only expanded Quarry Bank and extended his mercantile activities, but he constructed an empire of five cotton spinning and weaving mills, employing more than 2,000 people. Expansion was largely concentrated in the early 1820s, when rising profit margins encouraged investment in the industry as a whole. Its extent, however, far exceeded that of the average firm, which remained comparatively modest in scale.

Market conditions, whilst providing an inducement to business expansion, do not alone explain the growth of Samuel Greg and Company. Greg wanted to guarantee his sons' future, by providing each with a mill. It was thus no coincidence that when each son finished his education and joined Samuel in the firm, an additional mill was acquired. Aided by an experienced manager, the young men each took responsibility for a mill. In this way, Samuel tried to ensure that his sons could supplement their business knowledge, in preparation for the day when the firm became their property. Invaluable in ensuring continued family control of such a large enterprise, this policy had its limitations and, even before 1834, the costs of nepotism were apparent. Moreover, there were inevitable, wearing conflicts between an increasingly stubborn old man and his sons.

Samuel Greg and Company was one of the relatively few large cotton firms in the second quarter of the nineteenth century. Its capacity to grow was a direct result of long establishment, family connections and the extensive wealth of its proprietor. The combination of a high level of retained profits, easy access to short-term credit and loans and a large 'non-cotton' income, facilitated the growth of this family firm. That it was through multi-plant development was to be expected, since constraints of a personal, technological and managerial nature precluded expanding Quarry Bank too far. Thus, alternative sites had to be found and developed.

I The growth of Samuel Greg and Company

The Napoleonic War period had seen relatively slow investment in the cotton industry because of market uncertainty; potential profit margins were high, but so were the risks involved. During the subsequent 15 years there was a significant growth in the cotton industry. It emerged, by 1830, at the forefront of the British economy – a position it was to occupy until 1890.[1] Demand was a major stimulant to the cotton industry between 1815 and 1834. Although the home market for cotton goods remained relatively stagnant, exports grew signficantly, especially those to Latin America and India. Exports of cotton piece goods more than doubled between 1815 and 1834, whilst those of thread grew from 0.2 million lb in 1815 to 2.3 million lb in 1834. Twist and yarn exports also increased from 9 million lb in 1815 to reach 76 million lb in 1834.[2] Not only was the trade in cotton goods growing in absolute terms but it occupied an increasingly important position in Britain's overseas trade. From 1831 to 1850 on average, cotton goods, therefore, made up 45 per cent of exports.[3]

Expansion of the cotton industry did not occur suddenly. The ending of the war with France undoubtedly reduced uncertainty and allowed raw cotton prices to fall, but the improved market conditions, which encouraged investment, were not instantaneous. Whilst cotton prices fell from an average of 17.97d during the years 1801 to 1815 and to 15.48d between 1816 and 1821, yarn prices fell more rapidly and thus eroded profit margins.[4] The post-war slump reached its nadir in 1819, in which year one of Samuel Greg's nephews complained ' . . . in Manchester the manufacturers are in a dreadful state and many weavers will be thrown out of employ – low rates of profit will not maintain the people and I fear for the next two years'.[5] Fortunately, there was a recovery, although it was not sustained until 1821. There followed what some historians have described as the first cyclical boom in the history of the British economy. Investment in public utilities and foreign bonds grew at the same time as industrial investment. By 1824 the nation was caught in a wave of feverish speculation which culminated in the financial crisis of 1825.

In the cotton industry a few millowners, including Samuel Greg, began investing in new plant after 1819. In 1815 Greg sold his Peter

Street mule mill to Peter Ewart and terminated their partnership. Four years later he embarked on a massive investment programme which transformed his firm into one of the industry's integrated giants. Growth was on two levels. In 1819 work began on the building and equipping of a new four-storey mill at Quarry Bank, whilst additional mills elsewhere in Cheshire and Lancashire were acquired. At Styal, a massive 100-horse-power water wheel was built. The wheel, which weighed 44 tons and was 32 feet in diameter and 21 feet wide, was installed[6] by Thomas Hewes, a leading wheelwright responsible for many of the new generation of large iron water wheels. Housed in a deep chamber underneath the new mill, the wheel had ' . . . few equals in the country in point of size and efficiency . . . [its] . . . slow and stately revolution seems to be the very embodiment of power and dignity and it had been the pride of the owner to exhibit and the wonder of the spectator to behold . . . '[7] The tail water was taken off by a tunnel, which emerged three-quarters of a mile downstream and was itself a remarkable piece of engineering. As a result of the new wheel, spindlage could be increased. Gradually during the 1820s, as Table 3.1 shows, the number of spindles employed at Quarry Bank grew by 130%, the optimum number for the size of the wheel being reached in 1831. As spindlage increased, so too did the numbers employed, which grew from 252 to 346.[8] As a consequence, 42 new cottages were built during the 1820s, along with a chapel, a school and a shop. Thus Styal's growth mirrored the growth of Quarry Bank. The long double row of Oak Cottages all had their own gardens and most had cellars, intended originally for hand-looms though they were never used for this purpose.

Expansion at Quarry Bank was confined to spinning. Other mills were being added to Samuel Greg and Company, which combined spinning and weaving. The first new mill to come into the Greg empire was Low Mill, Caton, near Lancaster. This stone-built, coarse spinning mill dated from 1784 and was powered, somewhat erratically, by the River Lune. Low Mill was owned by Greg's brother-in-law, Thomas Hodgson. Between 1813 and 1815 Hodgson's son, Isaac, had been a partner in the mercantile branch of Samuel Greg and Company.[9] The enterprise had incurred heavy losses whilst trading in Spain. It was to cover Isaac Hodgson's share of these losses that Low Mill was finally passed to Greg in 1817 – after Thomas Hodgson's death, although agreement had been reached the previous year when improvements began.[10] Low Mill, a small mill, was valued at £3,000 (including machinery)[11] and was desperately in need of renovation. The building itself was small and cramped, with obsolete machinery.

Table 3.1 *Quarry Bank spindlage, 1817–31*

Date	Spindlage
1817	4,512
September 1818	4,476
March 1819	4,704
September 1819	5,052
March 1820	5,200
September 1820	5,450
March 1821	6,246
September 1821	7,400
March 1822	8,500
September 1822	8,686
March 1823	9,600
1831	10,846

Sources: MCL C5/1/2/3, partnership accounts; MCL C5/1/1/3, John Kennedy and Peter Ewart's valuation of Quarry Bank in 1831.

Moreover, the power supplied by the River Lune was uncertain and the site subject to flooding.

For the Caton Mill to be a profitable addition to the firm, extensive modernisation was necessary. Work began in 1817 and over the next fourteen years the mill was enlarged, new machinery installed and a Hewes water wheel added. To combat the erratic water power, a 20-horse-power Boulton and Watt steam engine was installed.[12] Despite these improvements, Low Mill was not a viable proposition on its own. Distance from the main commercial centres increased transport costs, whilst even with the new engine, time lost through flooding remained high. Rather than sell the mill at a loss, Greg decided to run it in tandem with a mill in nearby Lancaster.

Cotton spinning had barely touched Lancaster, so there were few properties available. In 1822, however, Greg found the ideal site, when he bought a small ex-sailcloth mill and a few cottages. The mill, situated on Moor Lane, was adjacent to the canal, on a hill on the east side of the town, surrounded by plenty of space for expansion. In 1823, Greg began equipping the empty shell and, two years later, started extending it. The work was completed in 1826 and, by the time it was working at full capacity in 1832, it was the largest mill in the firm.[13] Using warps from Low Mill and weft produced on site, the steam-powered Moor Lane Mill concentrated on velveteen production.

The acquisition of Moor Lane Mill was closely followed by the

Table 3.2 *Samuel Greg and Company, 1833*

Name of mill	Number employed	Fixed capital (£)	Floating capital (£)	Total production (lb)	
				Yarn market	Cloth market
Styal	380	26,000	18,000	870,000	—
Caton	150	10,000	7,000	363,000	—
Lancaster	560	25,000	20,000	—	733,000
Bury	544	37,000	25,000	—	740,000
Bollington	450	n.a.	n.a.	n.a.	n.a.
Totals	2,084	98,000	70,000	1,233,000 (0.6% of total yarn market)	1,473,000 (1.03% of total cloth market)

Sources: *Select committee on manufactures* . . . PP 1833 (690) VI, p. 685; *First report from the commissioners . . . relative to employment of children* . . . , PP 1833 (450) XX, pp. 34–5; *Supplementary reports . . . relative to the employment of children* . . . , Part II, PP 1834 (253) XX, pp. 150–2; T. Ellison, *The Cotton Trade of Great Britain* (new impression 1968), p. 68.

purchase of a large steam-driven spinning and weaving mill in Bury. In 1827, Greg bought Hudcar Mill from the executors of Thomas Haslam.[14] Lowerhouse Mill, Bollington, was the final addition to the Greg empire. The property was leased from the executors of Messrs Antrobus from 1832 until 1846, when it was purchased by Greg. Originally built for silk spinning, the mill was powered by a water wheel and a Boulton and Watt steam engine.[15] Like the Moor Lane mill, it was an empty shell in need of a great deal of work, which Samuel Greg Junior undertook during the subsequent two years.

As a result of the expansion Samuel Greg and Company's workforce grew tenfold between 1816 and 1833 to stand at over 2,000, as Table 3.2 shows. Yarn output at Quarry Bank reached 699,223 lb a year by 1826, more than twice the level reached in 1816. Growth there was thus far more spectacular than that for the industry as a whole, where raw cotton consumption expanded by 5.4% a year for the same period.[16] Through multi-plant development Samuel Greg and Company expanded from a relatively modest firm into a giant. Between 1820 and 1829 the firm's raw cotton consumption grew at a phenomenal 45% a year (over five times faster than that for the industry as a whole). From spinning just 0.4% of all yarn produced at the end of the Napoleonic Wars, by 1833 Samuel Greg and Company's yarn output rose to 0.6% of the total, while the firm wove 1.03% of all cloth.[17]

Recent research has concluded that despite the growing importance of the cotton industry and the significant expansion of spinning capacity in the 1820s, any increase in the overall level of concentration was imperceptible. Large firms, such as Samuel Greg and Company, were the exception rather than the rule. There were a few dozen giants who, like Samuel Greg and Company, used 100 horse power or more. In cotton spinning, for example, out of 975 firms almost half used less than 20 horse power, whilst only one-tenth had over 100 hands and very few more than 150. Moreover, many mills were multi-occupied, with floor space, power and sometimes machinery rented by very small operators.[18] A range of constraints – managerial, technological and social – explain the predominance of small firms during the period. This analysis highlights the growth of Samuel Greg and Company (and that of others like the Peels and M'Connel and Kennedy). Such exceptional expansion is worthy of explanation. In the first place it is interesting to speculate why Samuel Greg chose to begin expansion of Quarry Bank before the post-war slump had lifted. Secondly, the question arises of why he chose multi-plant development for subsequent growth during the decade. Finally, there is the problem of how such expansion was possible.

The market for cotton yarn was relatively depressed after the Napoleonic Wars, indeed until the early 1820s. Although much of the expansion of Samuel Greg and Company was undertaken during boom conditions after 1822, the development of Quarry Bank began in the very depths of the post-war slump. Such an apparently idiosyncratic decision is worthy of explanation. Unfortunately, Samuel Greg left no account of why he began expanding Quarry Bank so soon after the Napoleonic Wars. There are, however, several possible explanations. It may be that despite the slump Greg increased spinning capacity on the expectation that cotton yarn markets would become more buoyant. This is, however, unlikely to be the only explanation, nor does it indicate why output grew so significantly. Moreover, it assumes homogeneity in the coarse yarn market and excludes the possibility that Greg might have been facing exceptional conditions in a particular market.

Greg's decision to expand output at Quarry Bank becomes rational in the light of the markets which he served and the prices he could command. Much of the coarse yarn produced at Quarry Bank at this time was selling at Barnsley and Norwich, where it was almost certainly used in mixed linen and cotton cloths.[19] The dramatic expansion of linen cloth production, after 1816,[20] doubtless encouraged him to expand yarn output. Several years later his son, Robert

Hyde Greg, hinted that Quarry Bank yarn enjoyed a favoured position in these markets.[21] Just what this position was and how Greg gained it is unclear. In the same letter, however, Robert Hyde Greg stated that Quarry Bank yarns commanded prices which were on average ten per cent higher than their competitors.[22] A reputation for high quality and regularity of delivery almost certainly created this advantage. Additionally, since Greg (unlike many of his competitors) had his own mercantile organisation, he could differentiate Quarry Bank yarns with his customers. The higher prices which Quarry Bank yarns could attract gave an added incentive for expansion since they increased unit profits.

Business historians have accepted that even in the nineteenth century there were restraints on competition, and evidence of collusion.[23] In cotton yarns it has been shown that during the 1780s, Arkwright was usually the price leader, whilst at the finer end of the market there was widespread evidence of price fixing by a few large producers.[24] The implicit assumption for coarser yarns from the 1790s onwards, however, is that no firm was large enough or sufficiently specialised to derive any benefit from its position in the market. The foregoing discussion of Samuel Greg's situation in the post-Napoleonic Wars period illustrates that even in coarse yarns there was a high degree of specialisation, making it feasible for an established spinner to dominate specific, if narrow, yarn markets.

The question arises of why Greg should have chosen, in common with industrialists like Strutt and Arkwright, to expand via multi-plant development during the 1820s. There are several reasons why he chose this type of organisation, in preference to developing Quarry Bank further – a course which would, ostensibly, have led to substantial economies in the use of water power. The primary one is technological. Although Quarry Bank was a prime water site, there was a limit, given prevailing technology, to the level of power which could be taken from the River Bollin. That limit was reached with the installation of the new water wheel. Any additional power would have had to be provided by a steam engine or engines. Several hundred horse power was needed to operate the Gregs' other mills. To have generated the equivalent at Styal would have been prohibitively expensive. Steam engines provided up to 20 horse power in supplementary power at Styal. Running costs were high, however, and the distance from the coalfield inflated these further. In 1849, James Henshall – the Quarry Bank manager – calculated that the cost of running a 100-horse-power steam engine would exceed that of the wheel by £274 per annum.[25] Moreover, until the late 1820s, it was still not possible to build steam engines of more than 50 or 60 horse power,[26] so several would have been needed, inflating capital costs.

Even before the expansion of water power at Quarry Bank, Greg became embroiled in disputes with his neighbours concerning the effect which his activities had on other river users. In 1815 Mr Neild of nearby Ashley Mill made a claim for damages against Greg for interrupting his water supply. His attorney received an irate letter from Neild's solicitor arguing that:

It is impossible that Mr Greg could be in perfect ignorance of this complaint. Mr Greg has for years past so impounded the water that in dry seasons Mr Neild's Mill has been stopped every day until noon . . . If Mr Greg will make an offer of compensation, or will meet Mr Neild to confer on the subject, Mr Greg will find that Mr Neild is not intractable or unreasonable . . .[27]

Despite issuing threats of litigation, however, Neild ultimately decided to abandon the case because of the expense. Three years later Greg received further complaints concerning the dangerous state of a bridge near Pownall Hall that he had erected when, as a result of his weir, a ford had become impassable. His attorneys urged him to rebuild the bridge: a request with which he reluctantly complied.[28] Had he developed a giant factory on the Styal site, such legal wrangles would have been far more frequent.

Technological limitations were not the only constraints on the extensive development of the Styal site. Substantial growth of output at Styal would have increased capital expenditure on the village community, already a major item because of the need to import numerous workers. As it was, by developing a series of different sites, two of which were in towns, Greg was saved this outlay. The managerial benefits of multi-plant development almost certainly outweighed the economies of a large, single site. On the single site fewer managers were required, creating a saving in salaries, but the relationship between employer and employed became more tenuous. As a paternalist, Greg preferred the close contact which developed between his employees and his sons on each site rather than the relative impersonality of a vast plant. A further constraint on the expansion of Quarry Bank was locational. The mill was built in a deep, steep-sided valley. Possibilities for further building were thus severely limited, especially as parts of the remaining land were subject to flooding. Of course, had Greg really wanted to extend output there, he could have built new plant close to the village, on the flat land above the cleft Bollin Valley. His reluctance was, in part at least, inspired by his personal attachment to a place he had made his home. Its tranquillity would have been spoilt by further expansion.

High levels of investment were needed to develop a business of this scale and, during the expansion, £124,280 was invested in buildings and machinery at Styal, Caton, Lancaster and Bury.[29] The use of water power at Styal significantly increased capital expenditure. This was because, although relatively cheap to run, if compared with a similarly powered steam engine, a large wheel was costly to install. At Styal, for example, the wheel inclusive of dam, leats and transmission system, cost £77 per unit of power.[30] Not only did the complexity of civil engineering increase with the size of the wheel, but as capacity increased so the need to provide additional housing grew. At Styal, for example, over £6,000 was spent on cottages.[31]

Some firms remained small during this period because they faced financial constraints,[32] finding profit retention an inadequate source of expansionary funds. It was common during the industrial revolution for manufacturers to retain profits to finance investment since, in an era of unlimited liability, long-term external funds, especially institutional, were hard to obtain; some expanded by taking new partners and all used the short-run credit offered by merchants and banks to free funds for fixed investment. Yet, few were able to grow to the extent of Samuel Greg and Company. Long establishment and accumulated wealth, together with a wide range of family connections, explain why Greg was able to outstrip most of his competitors.

The growth of Samuel Greg and Company was financed, principally, by profit and interest retention. An early start in a new industry, despite relative inefficiency, ensured that profit levels were high. In the Napoleonic Wars, the very uncertainty which encouraged Greg to diversify also enhanced his profit margins. Thus, between 1806 and 1815, returns on capital invested averaged 19.76% per annum.[33] Such returns, accumulated over a number of years, provided an excellent basis for expansion. Greg continued the policy during the post-war period and whilst returns were more modest, they did supplement the already sizeable reservoir of funds. Few later entrants or smaller operators had such a supply of funds at their disposal or were able to retain all manufacturing profits. Profit retention was a useful form of finance, but even the most frugal life-style required some support. Those without some alternative income would have to make withdrawals from profits. Greg's accumulated wealth and diversified income provide the key to his firm's expansion. Not only did his early start enable him to enjoy high profits over a long period, but by investing his inherited wealth outside the cotton industry in land, government stocks and shares, he was able to guarantee a substantial regular income. Occasionally, as when he

Table 3.3 *Samuel Greg's income from outside the cotton industry, 1822–32*

	Net non-cotton income (£)
1822–3	5,254
1823–4	4,089
1824–5	4,223
1825–6	4,982
1826–7	5,647
1827–8	n.a.
1828–9	5,559
1829–30	4,494
1830–1	4,873
1831–2	5,048

Source: QB, statement of Samuel Greg's income.

contributed to the Peruvian loan and when he became involved in his brother's firm, Greg Lindsay and Company, he made mistakes but, in general, his investment policy was wise, guaranteeing a substantial regular income. As Table 3.3 shows, this averaged £4,908 between 1822 and 1832. Thus, Greg was able to protect himself against periods of uncertainty, whilst maintaining a pleasant home, without any need to make withdrawals from manufacturing.

Greg's accumulated wealth came from inheritance and wise investment. Other factors, also the result of long establishment, further facilitated growth. His reliable reputation gave him ready access to short-term credit from merchants, builders and machine makers. Thus, current liabilities at Quarry Bank between 1819 and 1822, whilst the bulk of expenditure was taking place, averaged £22,932.[34] Moreover, his firm's stability and credit-worthiness were a major factor in securing a loan of £23,000 from the vendors of Hudcar Mill.[35] Greg was further helped by his position at the centre of an intricate web of Nonconformist family connections. His marriage to Hannah Lightbody had already been helpful.[36] Predictably, his children married into the Nonconformist business community, and so it was that the Gregs became intimately connected with such leading families as the Rathbones, Phillipses, Kennedys and Mellys, as Figure 3.1 shows. Of these, the Rathbones were the most beneficial. Well established as merchants in Liverpool, with long-standing business links with the Gregs, the family was the first known importer of American raw cotton. It is likely, though not proven, that they allowed the Gregs

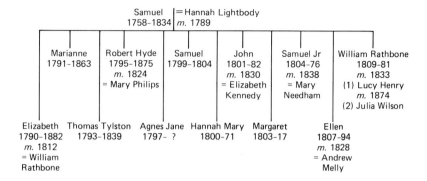

Figure 3.1 Samuel Greg's family tree

favourable credit terms for cotton, which would be a major contribution during a period of expansion. Ellen Greg's marriage to Andrew Melly, in 1828, was also significant. Melly joined his father-in-law as a sleeping partner at Hudcar Mill, bringing £5,772 as his capital balance.[37]

The expansion of Samuel Greg and Company was thus principally funded by profit retention and reliance upon short-term credit. In common with other giants in the cotton industry during the 1820s and 1830s, Samuel Greg and Company had been operating for many years, thus having a wide range of connections which eased the path of growth. A complex family network existed, linking many prominent firms in trade and industry. For those within this circle, such as the Gregs and M'Connel and Kennedy, financial constraints to the growth of their firms were few.

II Management and performance

Throughout the 1820s, the reins of control of Samuel Greg and Company remained firmly in the hands of its proprietor. However, Greg's four younger sons joined him in business between 1817 and 1830. Without them Greg would have had far less incentive to extend his business; indeed, they ensured prolonged family dominance of the conglomerate whilst it, as far as possible, guaranteed their future. Nevertheless, the relationship between Samuel Greg and his sons, – especially Robert – was often tense and when the inevitable policy disputes arose, they were bitter and prolonged.

Even before they had completed their formal education, Greg's sons began to learn the rudiments of business, so that they could enter the

Samuel Greg aged 60

family firm. Educated at Unitarian schools in Bristol and Nottingham, all Greg's sons proceeded to Edinburgh University. It was Hannah who emphasised the importance of education. She became infuriated when her husband subordinated learning to manufacturing and commerce. In 1816, she wrote to her daughter, Elizabeth ' . . . I rather hoped your father had forgotten or relinquished the idea of sending John to Liverpool this vacation, but yesterday, on his asking leave to have Mr Dalton's instruction this summer, your father told him he must learn his business . . .'[38] Samuel was keen, however, that they should all have the chance to travel as he had done, before settling down to regular work. Before they joined the firm in their early twenties, therefore, each went to Europe. The boys travelled as Samuel Greg and Company's representatives, meeting customers and investigating markets, as well as sight-seeing. This combination of

Robert Hyde Greg aged 30

business and pleasure both increased their commercial awareness and widened their horizons. That the scope of their journeys exceeded Samuel's own strictly utilitarian trips was the result of Hannah Greg's influence. She shrewdly realised that her sons were more likely to settle contentedly into the family firm if their youth had been stimulating. Moreover, she revered education for its own sake.

Robert Hyde Greg's descriptions of his visits to Europe are especially vivid. As well as reviewing the firm's trading arrangements there, he visited France, Italy, Greece and Turkey. Paris he dismissed in 1817 as cramped – his most enduring memory being of reckless driving: 'You have no idea [he wrote] of the danger of walking in the streets for there are so many carriages which drive fast and make a ceremony of running over anyone . . . '[39] He found Rome enthralling but overcrowded, whilst his visit to Greece inspired him to write several articles, which he later presented to the Manchester Literary and Philosophical Society. It was, however, the Alps which impressed him most. Travelling was dangerous and on precipitous tracks. He recalled ' . . . the path was never more than eight feet wide often not six and very much inclined . . . Our driver, however, far from being alarmed either for himself or his precious charges kept nodding off all the way, only opening his eyes to flog his horse or when a jog told him we were out of the track . . . '[40] Nevertheless, he was stunned by the scenery, which was ' . . . grand and novel, hills and valleys of ice and snow, bare and interspaced and covered with firs, the contrasts formed by these were very striking and increased by a singular sky, one half exceedingly bright, the other covered with the blackest cloud . . . '[41]

In 1817, shortly after completing this journey, Robert joined his father in the firm. He was followed by John in 1824, Samuel Jr in 1827 and William in 1830; thus the growth of the partnership mirrored that of manufacturing.[42] Just as Samuel Greg had been helped to business success by his uncles, so his sons were the main beneficiaries of his efforts. As each son joined him, Samuel transferred £5,000 to his account, giving each a share in the business.[43] Under the eye of an experienced manager, they completed their business apprenticeships, ultimately taking over a mill. Thus, Robert concentrated on Quarry Bank and the mercantile side of the business, with John overseeing the mills at Lancaster and Caton. Samuel Jr worked for a while with Robert at Styal, moving later to Bollington, and William was based at Bury. Although each son had an interest in running a mill, the profits from each were divided between all of them and, until 1832, Samuel Greg maintained overall control. Each received a share of profits, proportionate to his age and experience and consequent contribution to the firm. Thus, in 1831, Robert received 25 per cent of profits, John 15 per cent, with Samuel Jr and William each receiving 10 per cent; Samuel Sr retained the remaining 40 per cent.[44] In addition, 5 per cent interest was paid on capital holdings. The tradition of profit retention in manufacturing was maintained, since the brothers could make withdrawals from the mercantile concern, for their living expenses.

Despite these generous provisions, Samuel did not allow his sons to forget that the firm's success and reputation, especially that of Quarry Bank, were largely due to him and so he accordingly charged them a rent. This amounted to 5 per cent of the value of all buildings and 10 per cent on machinery.[45] It was a reasonable provision, in the circumstances, but an obvious source of friction. Conflicts of personality and interest between older and younger members of any partner-

Table 3.4 *Yarn output and mill margins at Quarry Bank, 1819–31*

	Yarn output (lb)	Raw cotton (pence per lb)	Yarn (pence per lb)	Mill margins (pence per lb)
1819–20	363,761	12.65	26.79	14.14
1820–21	381,700	11.54	20.76	9.22
1821–22	n.a.	10.13	19.37	9.24
1822–23	n.a.	9.62	19.19	9.57
1823–24	n.a.	8.97	19.53	10.56
1824–25	n.a.	9.02	18.85	9.83
1825–26	699,223	12.3	18.6	6.3
1826–27	692,888	7.03	13.43	6.4
1827–28	735,686	6.47	12.33	5.86
1828–29	820,964	6.56	n.a.	n.a.
1829–30	n.a.	5.43	11.16	5.73
1830–31	841,524	5.77	10.33	4.56

Note: the partnership accounts for Samuel Greg and Company run from September to March.
Source: MCL C5/1/2/4, partnership accounts.

ship are inevitable. When the protagonists in policy battles are father and son, even seemingly small disagreements take on monumental proportions. During much of the 1820s, whilst there were occasional undercurrents of tension, everything progressed smoothly. Greg was expanding his firm and his sons were finding their feet. By the end of the decade, however, there was growing animosity between Robert and his father. A forceful young man in his early thirties, Robert was beginning to resent the restrictions of being a junior partner in his father's business. He had ideas of his own, often more ambitious than those of the older man, and became increasingly critical of his father's policies, especially at Styal.

During the generally optimistic phase from 1822 until 1825, Robert had little to complain of. Output at Quarry Bank was rising consistently and buoyant markets meant that mill margins were high, as Table 3.4 shows. During the second half of the decade, however, mill margins were seriously eroded. The period was a bleak one for cotton spinners generally. The wave of investment which started in 1822 came to an abrupt end with the financial crisis of 1825. This led to a spate of bank failures. Repercussions were felt throughout the business community as credit was tightened or withdrawn.[46] Numerous cotton spinners failed, and for those who survived the future was bleak. The speculative investment of the early 1820s had created over-capacity. Yarn prices plummeted, eroding mill margins. With average revenues falling, spinners continued to take up new capacity created during the boom, thus generating a downward spiral in prices.[47] It was inevitably the coarse spinners, always reliant upon smaller margins than the fine yarn producers, who suffered most.

Quarry Bank was especially vulnerable. Dominance of specialist markets, far from giving the mill immunity from trade depression, may have proved a positive hindrance. The general collapse of yarn prices intensified. Competition, increasing the probability of market invasion, would force Greg to reduce his price. As Robert pointed out, '. . . our advantage from the engagement of our peculiar markets is daily reducing by competition and may be done away with at any moment by another spinner getting into the Barnsley and Norwich markets . . .'[48]

It seems that the capacity to charge higher than average prices in these markets in the past may have reduced the possibility of adaptation in the changed climate. Inflated prices created supernormal profits which removed the incentive to reduce costs significantly. Thus, whilst production costs did fall by over 40 per cent between 1825 and 1831, this did not compensate for falling yarn prices.[49] Moreover part of the advantage derived from quality. This led Greg to use more expensive cotton than was normal for 16s to 18s yarn. When competition intensified and he was forced to reduce his price to survive, profit margins fell and returns declined from 14.9% per annum, 1819–25, to 8.2% per annum in the subsequent six years.[50]

Robert believed that his father's lack of foresight was crippling the mill he stood to inherit. His policies were, he believed, extravagant and uncompetitive, whilst the very buildings made change and savings difficult. In a letter, written in May 1829, he wrote:

Something may [have been] done in reducing the number of overlookers if the mill had been properly made with two cardrooms instead of four, we might have done with twenty overlookers . . . This very constitution of the old mill make it worth less than a new one. The loss by short frames too is considerable. We have until lately thrown away something by using rather better cotton than necessary, for you never looked to the cost only quality with reference to cost, and for years I never went into the mill or to Quarry Bank [House] without you scolding about the bad quality of cotton and frequently told the overlookers to complain to me about it, instead of seeing that 7d cotton was used instead of 6¾d, when the latter was good enough. Had we been spinners of 160s, instead of 16s, you could not have been more particular about quality and less so about price . . . [51]

Robert's tirade against his father was in part justified. Arguably Quarry Bank would not have been viable as a separate entity and certainly was not attractive as an inheritance.

Declining margins at Quarry Bank led Robert to question the level of rent his father received. Satisfied that the payment of rent was reasonable, in principle, he was incensed at its level, which was based on Samuel's original expenditure rather than upon the mill's current value. Robert argued that, as a result of his father's inflated valuations, 'At the end of eight years I shall find I have given my time, attention and anxiety in buying cotton well, selling well and financing well, for nothing...'[52] Samuel eventually bowed to his son's pressure and agreed to an independent valuation, to allow for recalculation. This was carried out in 1831, when John Kennedy and Peter Ewart concluded that Greg had over-valued his fixed capital at Quarry Bank by 52 per cent and had consequently overcharged his sons. In the late 1820s, he had received approximately £4,420 per annum rent from his sons which, on the basis of the revaluations, should have been £2,500 per annum. No wonder Robert felt aggrieved![53]

Apart from his worries about profitability and the level of rent, Robert was concerned that his father did not own the freehold of the Quarry Bank site. To own the Styal property (in addition to the Oak Estate) would, he argued, safeguard the mill's future, which was precarious whilst reliant upon a life lease. In August 1829, he argued forcibly:

The mill property is a more important thing, and hanging by one life it will be an embarrassing one in many ways. You leave it to me and my brothers as worth perhaps £20,000 (without small machinery) ... If I fell from my horse tomorrow or die of bilious fever (not improbable to either of us if this thing pends much longer) you are £20,000 poorer at once.[54]

Samuel hesitated; he feared that the price of £62,643 was so high that it would render him a poor man for the rest of his life.[55] Given the extent of his commitments, he was probably right to be cautious, though Robert was irritated by his refusal to buy.

The other mills in Samuel Greg and Company had varying fortunes during the 1820s though overall, as Table 3.5 shows, returns were favourable. Predictably, Low Mill, Caton, faced similar problems to those encountered at Quarry Bank. A coarse spinning mill on the geographic periphery of the cotton industry, it incurred very high transport costs. These eroded profit margins so that although mill margins were, during the second half of the 1820s, slightly higher than those at Quarry Bank, returns were much lower, averaging only 1.8% per annum, 1826–31.[56]

It was, therefore, fortunate that Greg diversified his products during the 1820s, to include cloth. Although cloth prices did fall after 1825, this decline was far less severe than was encountered in yarn markets. As a result margins, especially in mills where spinning and

Table 3.5 *Return on capital invested in all the mills in Samuel Greg and Company, 1819–31*

	Return (%)
1819–20	14.8
1820–1	2.9
1821–2	13.4
1822–3	29.3
1823–4	28.5
1824–5	23.6
1825–6	−9.5
1826–7	0.4
1827–8	18.0
1828–9	9.7
1829–30	10.9
1830–1	16.0

Source: MCL C5/1/2/4–6, partnership accounts.

weaving were combined, stayed healthy. At Hudcar Mill Bury, for example, returns averaged 2s 6d per lb woven in 1828, whilst at Quarry Bank they were only 1s 5d per lb spun. Similarly at the Lancaster combined mill, whilst returns were more erratic than at Bury, performance proved acceptable.[57]

The question arises of why, given the poor performance at Styal, power looms were not installed. That Robert pressed for the change is highly probable since, in 1836, two years after his father's death, work began on weaving sheds. It could not have been, as has been suggested, that Samuel distrusted power looms,[58] as they were used in his other mills. A more likely explanation is that so soon after the rapid expansion of his firm he was not prepared to commit further funds, reasoning that, for a while at least, losses at Styal and Caton could be covered by profits at Bury and Lancaster. That he feared over-commitment is suggested in a letter a year before his death. He warned his son against ' . . . ye pushing things to ye utmost, the doing so is equally dangerous to prosperity as it is to peace of mind and your enjoyment of life and its blessings – all circumstances are not within our control, therefore pushing things to ye utmost is dangerous and frequently ruinous with your property and prospects'.[59]

Samuel was in his seventies, when, in 1832, an accident forced him to retire. Arguably he should have handed over the reins sooner, instead of retaining control for so long. He could then have avoided tiring disputes with his sons whilst, at the same time, better preparing them to run the business without him. In 1833 it was a tired, frustrated and saddened old man who wrote to Robert 'I feel my powers of body and mind rapidly in decay – I know that age and youth cannot feel and think alike – I see my opinions without influence and I wish to avoid the occasions of advancing any . . .'[60]

Had Samuel been less obsessive about his business and about retaining family control thereof, he might have realised that whilst Robert and John had the makings of competent businessmen, neither Samuel Jr nor William were well suited. For them their father's passports to business success simply led to discontent and unhappiness. Of William, whose talents were literary rather than practical, it was once said that his 'temperament was too sanguine in practical matters and . . . he had not that faculty of sustained attention which is the pith and marrow of success in a business such as his . . . '[61] Indeed, he himself was aware of his own shortcomings and dislike of the cotton industry when he confided in his elder sister, in 1833, writing:

I am bothered with every manner of calamities, boilers bursting, hands turning out, goods not selling and all the other ills that the flesh of a manufacturer is heir to. I am wearying after the country and ambition is forever extended within me. I wonder how long philosophy or indecision will induce me to continue the dog's life I am leading here. I never open a book . . . rise at 5.30 go to bed at 10 and toil like a galley slave all day.[62]

Samuel Jr, on the other hand, was an idealist who viewed his business as a social experiment, rather than a profit-making enterprise. When this experiment failed, he retired a broken man. The general business incompetence of these two severely increased the pressure on the partnership, especially after their father's death. Arguably, had the younger brothers not been forced into the firm, they would have been happier and the business more prosperous.

III Labour supply

The impact of the growth of Samuel Greg and Company and that of Quarry Bank on labour requirements was considerable. Table 3.6 shows that between 1816 and 1833 the firm's labour force grew almost tenfold, while at Quarry Bank there was a 50 per cent expansion. Parish apprentices played an important though diminishing role in the growth of Quarry Bank. Thus, while in 1816 36 per cent of the labour force was parish apprentices, by 1835 this percentage had declined to 20.[63] Instead of simply importing more and more parish children to facilitate the mill's growth, Greg sought increasingly to create a stable

Table 3.6 *Numbers employed in the cotton mills of Samuel Greg and Company, 1816–33*

Mill	1816	1833
Quarry Bank	252	380
Caton	–	150
Lancaster	–	560
Bury	–	544
Bollington	–	450
Totals	252	2,084

Sources: Report on the state of children . . . PP 1816 (397) iii, p. 374; Select committee on manufactures, shipping and commerce, PP 1833 (690) v, p. 685; Supplementary reports from the commissioners . . . relative to the employment of children . . . , Part ii, PP 1834 (253) xx, pp. 150–2.

labour base within Styal. Of the other mills only Low Mill Caton used apprentices, whilst local sources of labour were drawn upon at Bury and Lancaster.[64] There was a general decline in the use of parish apprentices in the cotton industry; indeed, Quarry Bank mill was one of the last mills to employ them. Legislation, patchy though it was, reduced the convenience and availability of parish children, whilst the declining use of water power reduced demand for them.

Parish apprentices were used less and less in the cotton industry, despite their early popularity. The decline began early in the nineteenth century and, by 1833, hardly any mill employed them.[65] Several factors explain this trend. Changes in legislation made them less attractive and less readily available, whilst movement in the location of industry reduced the need to import labour. Nevertheless, some millowners continued to employ them. Ultimately, it was the overall shift away from child labour in the cotton mills which led the last adherents to the system to abandon it.

A significant cause of the introduction of restrictive legislation to control the use of parish children in cotton mills was the abuse of the system by both millowners and parochial authorities alike. There was nothing new about parishes off-loading their surplus children. Maltreatment, excessive hours and malnutrition had always accompanied parish apprenticeship, but few individuals had had the ability to complain. It was the numbers involved and the distances they were sent which ultimately led to public disquiet. A minority of parishes, alarmed by accounts of excesses in cotton mills, found other outlets for their apprentices. Manchester was one of the earliest parishes to pursue this policy. In 1784 parochial authorities there forbade the apprenticeship of poor children into the cotton mills working nights.[66] Concern continued until 1803, when Sir Robert Peel, perhaps from conscience, introduced legislation for the protection of parish apprentices in cotton mills.[67]

Peel's Act extended the obligations of millowners with apprentices to include education and religious instruction. Additionally, it restricted to 12 the hours a day parish children could work and prohibited nightwork. In an attempt to guarantee compliance, Visitors were appointed to inspect conditions in mills with apprentices. Inspections, however, were rare and apparently cursory, and some mills were never visited.[68] It took 14 years and several false starts for any further controls to be introduced. In 1816, London parishes were forbidden to apprentice children more than 40 miles distant. This measure was designed to avoid some of the worst abuses of a system which allowed parishes to off-load their children so far away that officers rarely checked on their welfare. The legislation successfully dried up the supply of London children to cotton mills, though by 1816 the character and scale of demand had changed significantly. Those who still required apprentices simply turned to other parishes. Ironically, London's poor children were almost certainly worse off. Subsequent bindings were increasingly into the sweat-shops of the London clothing trades.[69] In these they frequently suffered horrors infinitely worse than in the cotton mills.

Legislation made parish children less convenient and more restricted in their supply. As a result, many employers reduced their reliance on them. The gradual decline in the importance of water power is another reason why the system became less widely used. The increasing use of steam engines meant that by 1816 mills were built '... not only as formerly on the banks of streams, but in the midst of populous towns and instead of parish apprentices being sought after, the children of the surrounding poor were preferred'.[70] Even this movement to towns may have been partially influenced by legislation. Restricting the hours one class of child could work meant that another class was more suitable. Only parish apprentices were affected by the new legislation; the hours which could be worked by free children were, at first, unregulated. Unless a large community had developed around a rural mill, it was unlikely that an adequate supply of free children would be forthcoming. This made movement to towns rational.

Few, if any, millowners relied entirely upon parish apprentices by 1816, though some continued to be used, primarily as a supplement mainly (though not exclusively) on exceptional water sites, such as Quarry Bank. Children were brought to Styal from Liverpool when the London supply dried up. Greg was, however, increasingly keen to create a permanent labour force as child labour became less convenient. With this in mind he added 42 extra cottages in the 1820s as well as a chapel, shop and school.[71] Increasingly ex-apprentices were given long-term employment as the family found that ' . . . the best families for good conduct have sprung from this source'.[72] As a result, by 1833, W. R. Greg asserted that ex-apprentices 'almost always marry, very often amongst themselves and remain with us as workmen'.[73] Contract labour (often whole families) was also recruited from amongst local poor and slowly a stable, permanent workforce was created, though it was not until 1847 that parish apprentices ceased to be used.[74]

IV Marketing

In contrast to manufacturing, between 1815 and 1834, the scale and scope of Samuel Greg's marketing activities diminished. This was the inevitable and prudent consequence of so much capital and effort being devoted to expanding spinning and developing weaving.

Contraction was not immediate. Despite the heavy debts and losses of the Napoleonic Wars, Greg continued to sell cloth, both his own and that of others, abroad at his own risk. This proved almost as hazardous as it had been before 1815. Between 1819 and 1822 the firm accumulated further losses totalling nearly £13,000, mainly in Europe.[75] The speculative boom of 1822–5 provided some respite, but the firm continued to be troubled by heavy bad debts until 1829. Greg was persuaded to abandon foreign business except on a commission basis. This meant that it was the producer – rather than Samuel Greg and Company – who took the risk. The change of policy was successful and the firm made profits averaging £2,410 per annum between 1829 and 1840.[76] Increasingly, however, although the firm continued to deal in a minor way in raw cotton and to act on behalf of other manufacturers, Samuel Greg and Company of Manchester became the servant of the Greg mills, all other business becoming strictly subsidiary. This relationship was preserved until late in the nineteenth century.

V An assessment of Samuel Greg

In June 1834, Samuel Greg died after what can only be described as a long and successful career in the cotton industry. Lucky in his inheritance, his contacts and in most of his business decisions, his achievements were considerable. Aware of the need to protect himself against uncertainty, he was none the less dynamic and adventurous – traits which made him one of the leaders of the cotton industry. With the help of his sons he developed a cotton spinning and weaving empire so large that even foreign visitors commented on it. Thus, Faucher observed that '. . . the firm of Samuel Greg and Company . . . holds first rank among the manufacturers. It consumes annually nearly four million pounds weight in cotton, possesses five factories, four thousand power looms and employs more than two thousand people at Bury, Bollington, Caton, Lancaster and Wilmslow.'[77] Added to this was, of course, a substantial mercantile concern.

Not only was Samuel Greg and Company large, it was, despite a decline in the late 1820s, also profitable; overall returns averaged 13.2% per annum between 1819 and 1831. At a time when many of their competitors were struggling, this was a very favourable result. The Ashworths at New Eagley, for example, only reaped an average return of 4.7% between 1818 and 1831.[78] Samuel Greg's career was not without mistakes. His delay in installing power looms at Quarry Bank was misguided, though understandable. His marketing policies were often risky and he incurred losses so great in that branch that a small firm would have been bankrupted. He, nevertheless, made maximum use of all opportunities and succeeded in establishing a vast and flourishing business.

There remains the question of motivation, the driving force which encouraged him to strive after wealth. To Adam Smith, the driving force behind most entrepreneurs was simple. It was the prospect of the 'consideration and good fortune which wait upon riches', whilst Malthus – who echoed these views twenty years later – added that most also wanted to make 'a permanent provision for a family'.[79] More recently, historians have confirmed these ideas. They have argued that for most entrepreneurs the main attraction of the wealth which came with business success was the accompanying prestige, when fortunes were used to purchase land. In eighteenth-century Britain, whilst land remained the traditional basis of status, it was a society which was sufficiently mobile to allow position to be purchased.[80] Unlike the rest of Europe at this time, where birth alone bestowed prestige, in Britain those who could afford to buy land ultimately enjoyed social acceptance. For the self-made man, struggling to gain a foothold, this prospect almost certainly encouraged his efforts. The impressive list of early industrialists, including Arkwright, Strutt, Peel and Wedgwood, all of whom bought properties, provides confirmation of this.[81] For some, land and the desire for social standing was enough to make them, or their sons, abandon business and commerce in favour of a more leisured existence. For those, however, who were wealthy at the beginning of the industrial revolution and became wealthier because of it, the picture should be modified. These men were often established merchants and were not clawing their way up the tortuous ladder of success. Many had considerable reputations at the beginning of the industrial revolution, which they used as a basis of success as factory owners. Within the business communities of Manchester and Leeds, and other provincial centres, there emerged a social hierarchy quite divorced from the traditional ranks. A close-knit network was dominated by established Nonconformist mercantile families – the aristocracy of the commercial world. Members of these families enjoyed great social cachet within their own circle and possessed sufficient standing to ignore traditional prestige. Indeed, it was their position in their community which ensured that their businesses continued to flourish and expand. It is true that they bought land and travelled abroad, but their activities lacked the desperation of the newly rich. For them land was primarily an investment which might, as a bonus, increase prestige.[82] In general they combined the fruits of their wealth with an active business career, showing little inclination to join the establishment.

Samuel Greg's was not a story of a man rising from comparative obscurity and poverty to head a massive business empire. Instead, he began his career in an already established firm. Valuable family connections not only ensured that his enterprises flourished, but guaranteed his position in Manchester. There is very little evidence to suggest he had any desire to join the ranks of the establishment: instead his main aim was to provide for his numerous children and enable them to enjoy the same advantages as he had. Certainly he invested in land, but more to generate income and to provide an insurance through diversity than to gain prestige.[83]

೫೫೫

The middle years, 1834–1870

The forty years after Samuel Greg's death were a period of consolidation for the cotton industry. Output expanded apace in response to a growth in markets at home and abroad. Yarn output more than doubled between 1831 and 1851, doubling again to reach 1,1009 million lb per annum by 1871. There was an even more significant rise in the production of cloth. In 1829–31 annual output averaged 153 million lb, by 1869–71 it had reached 828 million lb.[1] By the 1850s, the cotton industry had for the first time surpassed wool in the home trade. At the same time, demand for British cotton manufacturers from North America, Australia, Asia and the Levant grew at an impressive rate. The growth in demand for yarn was greatest in the home market – especially in such specialist sectors as lace and sewing cotton. Cloth, on the other hand, whilst experiencing increased demand at home, faced dramatically expanding export markets. Cotton's share of British trade also grew. Thus, by 1860, 17 per cent of the value of imports was made up of raw cotton, while cotton manufacturers accounted for 38.3% of the value of domestic exports.[2] Although productivity improved, the increase in output was accompanied by a significant rise in spindlage, power loomage and the numbers employed in the industry. Between 1834 and 1878 cotton factory employment rose by 104 per cent. Spindlage and the number of power looms grew even more markedly. Between 1819 and 1821 spindlage totalled 7 million; by 1878 there were 44.2 million spindles in use in the industry. Similarly, during the same period, the number of power looms rose from 14,000 to 515,000.[3]

Despite the continued growth of output, the cotton industry experienced mixed fortunes. There were several extended periods of exceptional prosperity and expansion, but in 1841–2 and 1861–5 depression reached unprecedented depths. Concurrently, changes in the industry's structure occurred as power weaving became more and more

common. At the same time, the eclipse of water by steam as the major
source of motive power helped to stimulate the growing localisation of
the industry within Lancashire. The typical firm, however, remained
the small family partnership. There was no joint stock boom in the
industry until the limited liability legislation of the 1860s. Even then,
many of the firms which acquired 'limited' status were what became
known as 'private limiteds'. These were established family partnerships, seeking the protection of the new legislation.

For the Greg brothers, the middle years of the nineteenth century
lacked the prosperity and optimism of earlier decades. They witnessed, indeed precipitated, the disintegration of their father's
empire, within seven years of his death. The vast conglomerate lacked
direction. It fell to Robert Hyde Greg to provide leadership. The task of
directing the diverse concern and of mediating between his brothers,
however, proved both unrewarding and exhausting. In 1841, on
Robert's instructions, Samuel Greg and Company was disbanded,
each brother taking the mill for which he had been responsible.

With the demise of Samuel Greg's empire came a relative decline in
the family's position at the forefront of the cotton industry. Nevertheless, Robert and John – competent rather than inspired businessmen –
were able, with the help of their sons, to steer their mills successfully
through the century. Robert even expanded his interests. Their
younger brothers were, however, less fortunate. Their business
careers were short-lived and, by 1850, both had withdrawn from the
cotton industry, their struggling mills sold. By the time of John Greg's
retirement in 1864, and Robert's in 1870, the nature of the cotton
industry had changed. Concentration of the industry within a fairly
small area of Lancashire, close to the coalfield and within easy reach of
Manchester and Liverpool, made those mills on the periphery with
heavy transport costs less and less competitive. This persuaded John
Greg to sell his two mills at Lancaster and Caton during the 1860s.
Both Quarry Bank and Lowerhouse were much closer to the nucleus of
the industry and performed comparatively well. There were, nevertheless, limitations at Quarry Bank. As a result, Robert Hyde Greg
rented a spinning and doubling mill at Calver, in Derbyshire, and built
another two (only one for his own use) on his Reddish estate, near
Stockport in Cheshire. With competent management, Calver might
have thrived. As it was, Robert Philips Greg, who lacked even a grain
of business instinct, ran it, and it proved a dismal failure. By contrast
Albert Mill, Reddish, run by Robert Hyde Greg himself with the help
of Henry, his third son, was to guarantee the family's position into the
twentieth century. Larger, more specialised and more modern than

Table 4.1 *Net profits in Samuel Greg and Company (£), 1831–41*

	Quarry Bank Styal	Low Mill Caton	Moor Lane Lancaster	Hudcar Mill Bury	Lowerhouse Mill Bollington	Total
1831–2	−1,175	n.a.	+7,992	+9,210	—	+16,027
1832–3	−2,700	+211	+2,092	+3,051	—	+2,654
1833–4	−3,566	−1,020	−1,792	−914	−1,588	−8,880
1834–5	+2,206	+994	+2,557	+3,366	−254	+8,869
1835–6	+1,586	+1,831	+1,253	−301	−3,428	+941
1836–7	+190	+1,216	+2,599	−1,190	+6,364	+9,179
1837–8	−423	+943	−676	−2,851	+2,924	−83
1838–9	+534	−439	+228	−1,300	+36	−941
1839–40	−2,682	+277	−3,414	−5,095	−4,942	−15,856
1840–1	+3,290	+1,711	−456	+1,266	+87	+5,898
Average per annum	−274	+636	+1,038	+524	−100	+1,780

Source: 'Memoranda of Greg concerns, 1750–1867'

Quarry Bank, Albert Mill could compete successfully in a changing environment.

I The demise of Samuel Greg and Company

For seven years after Samuel Greg's death his sons maintained a formal partnership agreement. While each was responsible for a mill, Robert also took charge of marketing and general guidance of the partnership. They shared the accumulated profits of the conglomerate. The Gregs found the 1830s a trying decade; profits at all mills were meagre, as Table 4.1 shows. Without the profits from marketing and the rents they received from inherited land, the brothers would have had little to live on. The mills at Lancaster and Caton performed relatively well, but Lowerhouse's fortunes were variable and Quarry Bank was struggling. At Hudcar Mill, easily the most successful component of the firm in the late 1820s, profits became a rarity.

From the start, Robert was keen to restore Quarry Bank's profitability, perceiving that its poor performance was a drain on the company and on his brothers. The decline in Quarry Bank's fortunes stemmed, he believed, from concentration on spinning. Salvation, he concluded, lay in diversification, so he added power weaving. Work began in 1836 and by 1838 two weaving sheds and a cloth warehouse were completed at a cost of £1,089. The weaving sheds of two and four storeys, with cellars, ultimately housed 305 looms. Supplementary power was provided by a 20-horse-power steam engine.[4] The exercise was successful and Quarry Bank subsequently became '... profitable and pulled through the ups and downs of cotton with credit and profit ...'[5]

Fire was a major hazard in early cotton mills. A high proportion of mill blazes started in scutching rooms, where oil, raw cotton and static electricity often proved to be a lethal combination. Effective fireproofing and sprinkler systems came only slowly, as a result of pressure from insurance companies. By the 1830s, however, a few iron-framed buildings were being constructed and some millowners sought to protect at least the more vulnerable parts of their mills. It was this consideration which persuaded Robert Hyde Greg to add a fireproof scutching room at Quarry Bank, in 1836. Ironically, while this work was in progress, a serious fire almost destroyed Low Mill Caton. The fire began in the early hours of 16 December 1837. The alarm was raised promptly, but as there was no fire engine in the village, one had to be brought from Lancaster. By the time it arrived, much of the old mill, its machinery and stocks had been destroyed. The floors had collapsed, leaving only a precarious external shell. Fortunately, the newer north end of the mill and the steam engine were saved. Damage was estimated at between £12,000 and £15,000, but the firm only received £5,370 compensation from their insurance company.[6] The consequences of the fire for John Greg and his partners and employees were potentially serious. With Low Mill at a standstill, production at the Lancaster mill was also threatened with interruption or with the use of costly supplementary yarn. Either way, the partnership faced serious losses and the operatives the loss of their jobs. The firm's plight was recognised by two local firms, Messrs Wright of Ingleton and Gregson and Mason of Lancaster.[7] They placed their mills at the Gregs' disposal at night, whilst Low Mill was rebuilt. John Greg took the opportunity to modernise the mill, adding power looms, though it continued to supply the Lancaster mill with warps.[8]

Had the partnership's difficulties been restricted to the rejuvenation of Quarry Bank and the fire at Low Mill, it might have survived. Neither Lowerhouse nor Hudcar thrived, however, the shortcomings of both Samuel Jr and William becoming all too apparent. At Hudcar Mill, for example, William had, at first, been guided by an experienced manager, John Holme. In 1832 Holme went to Bollington to help Samuel Jr. It was no coincidence that from then on Hudcar Mill deteriorated.[9] Samuel Jr, on the other hand, was much more interested in developing his factory colony than in his mill's profitability and, unbeknown to his brothers, was accumulating serious debts.

It was Robert who felt the pressure most. Entrusted by his father with overall responsibility for the partnership, he tried in vain to hold it together. There would have been fewer problems had the mills been closer together and the brothers equally committed to the firm. As it was, their dispersion, combined with the varying abilities and clashing temperaments of the brothers, made long-term unity impossible. In some ways, Robert was the last person who should have been obliged to guide the partnership. An obsessively meticulous man, he worked incessantly to support the foundering firm. Moreover, at the same time he was involved in the anti-Corn Law campaign, a cause to which he devoted a great deal of time. The strain proved too great and, by 1839, he was suffering from severe headaches and was on the verge of a nervous breakdown. He went abroad for a complete rest and concluded there was no future for the partnership. Recalling the period without any pleasure, he wrote in his journal:

Until going abroad in the spring of 1839, I have given most active superintendence to all concerns, spending for many years three long days weekly at Manchester, devoting minute attention not only to sales and financing, but scrutiny of quality of goods, correspondence with five or six mills and buying of cotton. All this with the anxieties of the disastrous time commencing with 1837 was almost too much . . .[10]

Samuel Greg and Company was broken up in 1841, just seven years after the death of its founder. To Samuel it had been a family dynasty by which he could support his wife and children and over which, until 1832, he exerted sole authority. The absence of this overriding control – financial, managerial and psychological – made the partnership unworkable and inappropriate. Samuel may have given Robert responsibility for the concern, but he could not endow him with the authority of a father over his sons. Without Samuel's guidance, therefore, the partnership was doomed. It became a managerial structure quite unequal to its task. Family businesses are an admirable form of organisation during the early stages of industrialisation. Within them are, however, certain limitations. Whilst adequate funds can generally be found, especially within established commercial families, nepotism does not always guarantee a suitable succession. Moreover, as partnerships grow they can become cumbersome and unmanageable, especially if lacking suitable leadership.

Although the manufacturing partnership was terminated in 1841, the brothers all retained an interest in the marketing concern until 1844,[11] and when Samuel Jr and William ran into difficulties in the late 1840s, Robert and John came to their rescue. If the 1830s had been troubled for all the Gregs, the 1840s were disastrous for the two younger brothers. All the mills suffered during the violent depression of 1841–2. During the last nine months of the partnership, losses totalling £11,453 were incurred.[12] Robert and John were soon to nurse their mills back to prosperity but Lowerhouse and Hudcar never fully recovered.

By his wife's testimony, Samuel Jr, obsessed by his factory colony at Bollington, never paid much attention to profits.[13] Convinced that his mission was to improve the condition of working people, he ignored their true interests. Pleasant working conditions, good housing and recreational facilities were admirable, but they were costly and relied on the profitability of the mill. Furthermore, operatives were ultimately interested in secure employment and this was threatened by Samuel Jr's distractions.[14] He amassed phenomenal debts of around £32,000 by 1847.[15] A strike at Lowerhouse in 1846, which he saw as a betrayal of trust, hastened his withdrawal from business. Nevertheless, it is unlikely that he could have staved off bankruptcy, unaided, had he stayed. He retired, a broken man, leaving his brothers to salvage the mill. For many years he became a virtual recluse, showing no further interest in the cotton industry.

It was difficult and expensive to unravel the complex finances of the mill, to meet Samuel's debts and restore the concern to efficiency and profitability. Samuel's brothers were keen to save him from bankruptcy. This was not only for his own sake but, presumably, because in a world where family ties remained important, it would have reflected badly upon their credit-worthiness. Although all three brothers were involved in revitalising Lowerhouse Mill, it was William, Samuel's closest companion as a boy, who was persuaded to go to Bollington in 1847, abandoning Bury. Shocked by what he found, he tried hard to save the mill.[16] By 1850 he believed he had achieved a measure of success, when John expressed an interest in taking the mill. William was appalled. Not only had he worked hard, but he had neglected his own mill for the sake of his brother's. His anger at John's intentions was clear when he wrote to Robert:

I have for sometime had a suspicion that John had an eye on Bollington, but I banished it as unjust to him to entertain. Why did he not take it in 1847 as I urged him to do instead of sending me there? I went there, as he knows, very reluctantly; I was frightened at the state of the concern, and the amount of Sam's liabilities – but he was not disposed to do anything himself, so I was obliged and did it in fear and trembling . . . I went to Bollington, transferred there all my interests and affections, gave myself up to it entirely and, after two years labour . . . I have brought it into good working condition. Bury, of course, suffered irretrievably both in credit and machinery during the time it was standing . . . and now John proposes to leave me the mill which on his advice I relinquished and take the one which has had the benefit of my labour for nearly 3 years . . . Really, this seems to me something which coming from a brother I do not like to characterize . . . [17]

It is hard to tell how accurate William was in his perception of his achievements at Bollington. Always diligent, he had little real appreciation of business problems and his own mill had been ailing for many years. Indeed, in 1842 his wife Lucy's poor health had forced him to move to Ambleside and spend only half his time at Bury. Nevertheless, it seems strange that John wanted him to go to Bollington if he lacked all ability. Whatever the truth behind the episode, William sold Hudcar Mill in 1850 for £17,000, a fraction of what his father had paid for it in 1828, and John took Lowerhouse. Whether the rift between the two brothers ever healed is unclear but, like his brother Samuel, William abandoned the cotton industry. After a short period of writing in the Lake District, he moved to London where he joined the Civil Service, working first in the Board of Customs and then as Controller of the Stationery Office, until his retirement in 1877. He found the work little more to his taste than being a millowner, but was rather more successful at it. In May 1856 he wrote to a friend:

My position everyone but myself seems to think most enviable. I contrast Lower Thames Street with The Craig [his Lakeland home] and my heart sinks in my shoes. The attendance is onerous; the actual work is not. It seems to be a place where a man may grow old comfortably. There is a good salary (nominally £1,200) and a liberal Retiring allowance when you are worked out. A board every day ... varied only by the occasional tours of inspection – sounds horrible slavery to a man accustomed to wander at his own free will ...[18]

As a result of the traumas of the 1840s, only two of Samuel Greg's sons remained in the cotton industry. The family's difficulties, however, were caused less by fluctuations in the industry's fortunes than by problems of personality. The depression of 1841–2 merely highlighted existing deficiencies. The Gregs' experience in the 1830s and 1840s illustrates the perennial problem of the family business – the frequent unsuitability and unwillingness of an entrepreneur's son to follow him into business. Yet, in an age when the unity of ownership and control within a firm was normal and when professional management was in its infancy, there were few alternatives.

John Greg retained his mills at Lancaster and Caton until the 1860s. Similarly, he continued to manage Bollington with the help of his son, Francis, until 1864. Francis and his elder brother, Albert, then converted it into a limited company – one of the wave of family limited companies which proliferated in the 1860s. Limited status barely changed the organisation of Lowerhouse Mill and the shareholders all came from within the family circle. They included members of the Greg, Rathbone and Melly families. The new legislation did not kill the family firm, it simply provided new protection.

II Performance of Robert Hyde Greg's mills, 1841–75

Relieved of the burden of guiding the partnership and, by 1850, of his brothers' financial worries, Robert worked hard to develop his own business, both in manufacturing and selling. He had a large family to provide for, as Figure 4.2 shows, and wanted his sons to become his partners, so he decided to expand. Robert began expanding his interests when he rented Calver Mill in Derbyshire and started work on two mills at Reddish. There were also major repairs to the Quarry Bank water wheel and efficiency was improved. Thus, by 1856, it generated 172 nominal horse power.[19]

Calver Mill, which was to be run by Robert Philips Greg, was a six-storeyed spinning and doubling mill, powered by two water

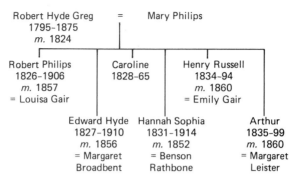

Figure 4.1 Robert Hyde Greg's family tree

wheels with a combined horse power of 140. The mill, which had once belonged to the Pares family (the Gregs' cousins) needed extensive modernisation. Between 1847 and 1864 £11,372 was spent on spinning and doubling machinery[20] for the production of doubled yarn, for sale in Manchester and locally in Leicester, Nottingham and Derby, where there was significant demand from lacemakers.

While Calver was being modernised, work was proceeding at Reddish. Robert and John, determined to improve the value of their estate, built two spinning and doubling mills, the Victoria and Albert, for two spinners – Bowlas and Ogden. Ogden failed shortly afterwards and for a while Robert ran Albert Mill in partnership with David Bowlas. Immediately, he extended the mill, doubling its size and adding a 50-horse-power steam engine. In 1853 Robert, in partnership with his son, Henry, took over entirely. By then the mill was larger than Quarry Bank and was worth £34,143. By 1870 a further £18,603 had been spent on Albert Mill.[21] New investment at Quarry Bank was on a much more modest scale and a little over £7,000 was spent between 1857 and 1870 by Robert and his son, Edward, mostly on machinery.[22] The mill's yarn output remained coarse and very little was sold, it being principally used within the company in cloth production.

At Quarry Bank, between 1840 and 1875, the major increase in output came when weaving capacity was taken up during the 1840s. Otherwise, as Table 4.2 shows, apart from cyclical fluctuations it remained relatively stable until 1875. Growth in the industry as a whole was, however, more spectacular, as suggested by the mill's declining share of total cloth output. During the 1820s and 1830s, the main strategy at Quarry Bank had been to increase revenue by expanding output. By the 1840s, however, water power had been

Table 4.2 *Quarry Bank, 1840–75*

	Spindlage	Loomage	Number Employed	Output (lb)		Share of cloth market (% of total cloth output)
				Yarn	Cloth	
1840	11,360	165	435	1,040,349	526,806	(not relevant)
1845	11,078	303	396	1,110,300	947,689	0.3
1850	10,838	284	377	855,399	720,169	0.2
1855	11,007	305	369	1,054,432	1,020,626	0.2
1860	11,014	299	365	988,538	946,705	0.1
1865	11,054	284	363	783,934	712,686	0.1
1870	10,704	252	356	1,091,302	1,075,889	0.07
1875	10,891	295	383	971,944	985,517	0.1

Note: Calculation of total cloth output is a crude estimate assuming cloth output was 67% of total raw cotton consumption (derived from T. Ellison, *The Cotton Trade* . . . , p. 69).
Sources: B. Mitchell and P. Deane, *Abstract of British Historical Statistics* (Cambridge 1962), p. 179; MCL C5/1/7/1–2, spinning and weaving production books; MCL C5/1/15/2–7, wages books.

Table 4.3 *Output of yarn and cloth at Quarry Bank, 1840–75 (lb per man/hour)*

	Yarn	National average	Cloth	National average
1840	0.91	n.a.	1.57	n.a.
1845	1.45	0.8	1.58	0.7
1850	1.60	n.a.	1.51	n.a.
1855	1.92	n.a.	1.87	n.a.
1860	1.80	1.2	1.75	n.a.
1865	1.38	n.a.	1.41	n.a.
1870	1.94	n.a.	2.09	n.a.
1875	2.14	1.9	2.15	1.5

Source: MCL C5/1/7/1–2, spinning and weaving production book; M. Blaug, 'The productivity of capital in the Lancashire cotton industry during the nineteenth century', *EcHR* 13 (1960), p. 36.

extended to its technical limit, whilst the comparatively high costs of using additional steam power in an area remote from the coalfield precluded any change in motive power. Thus, increasingly, emphasis was laid upon efficiency within existing capacity. There was a resultant steady increase in productivity of both spinners, except for the American Civil War period, as Table 4.3 shows.

This increase was achieved in spinning by the introduction of self-acting mules and by replacing water-frames with Darnforth throstles, both important labour-saving devices. In weaving, the improvement to productivity was much more modest than in spinning. This was largely because it was much easier to increase the number of spindles per operative than the number of looms. It is significant that, throughout, labour productivity was above the national average.[23]

Performance at Quarry Bank, Calver and Reddish varied. Both Quarry Bank and Reddish enjoyed similar fortunes for much of the 1850s and 1860s. Returns on capital owned for the two mills averaged 8.8 per cent per annum and 8.9 per cent per annum respectively between 1857 and 1870. Interestingly, however, Calver Mill, which was producing a very similar product to that spun at Reddish was noticeably less successful and encountered losses for many years, until it was given up in 1864.

The most testing phase for the Greg mills was the slump of 1861–5. This depression was very severe, with high levels of unemployment and short-time working in the cotton districts. It was once assumed that it was the simple result of a shortage of raw cotton created by the blockade of southern ports during the American Civil War. As a result, the depression was dubbed the 'Cotton Famine'. Recent research has revealed that the assumption of direct causality between the depression and a physical shortage of raw cotton is doubtful.[24] In the first place it seems that a depression in the cotton industry was inevitable, since the boom of the late 1850s had created over-capacity. Additionally, raw cotton prices rose less because of an *absolute* shortage of raw cotton than because the expectation of one led to speculation among dealers and some millowners. The position of many producers was aggravated by the growing substitution of inferior Indian cotton for American cotton from 1862, which led to soaring production costs. Since markets were dull, price rises were often inadequate to compensate for spiralling production costs, and profit margins were eroded. For those marginal firms with few reserves and little opportunity to reduce costs, the future was bleak. This was especially true for many of the more isolated country mills. At a distance from the commercial centres of Liverpool and Manchester, they already operated with inflated costs. The spiralling production costs of the early 1860s frequently sounded their death knell.

The spectre of the American Civil War alarmed Robert Hyde Greg. In May 1861 he wrote:

I am very uneasy about the prospects of business. We are about entering on very dangerous and difficult times, I fear, and the American affairs will be much more protracted and serious than at one time I thought . . . I am sorry I began any building at Norcliffe and now would not have laid out a penny in sinking money, everything being required . . .[25]

He was not above speculating in raw cotton and, in 1862, sold 325 bales of American and Surinam cotton at a profit of £1,752.[26] He was, however, nervous of the impact which uncertainty and soaring raw cotton prices would have on his mills and sales, and urged his sons to be cautious. Thus in 1861 he wrote:

As to what to do in business it is not easy to say. It is good advice when you cannot see your way to stand still . . . goods and yarns never follow a rapid rise of cotton from a fair medium price. All wait, necessarily, except a few making large speculative purchases at old prices . . . Between war with Europe and the state of matters in America no one can predict or limit the extent of possible mischief in the future.[27]

He was right, as Table 4.4 shows. Raw cotton prices did rise more rapidly than cloth prices. Production costs also rose. Waste levels increased substantially and unit labour costs rose with short-time

Table 4.4 *Raw cotton and cloth prices and mill margins at Quarry Bank,*
1857–65 (d per lb)

	Raw cotton	Cloth	Mill margins
1857	6.12	10.3	4.18
1858	5.35	11.03	5.68
1859	5.6	11.38	5.78
1860	4.72	11.79	7.07
1861	5.67	11.41	5.74
1862	7.9	15.21	7.31
1863	16.25	24.5	8.25
1864	18.2	26.55	8.35
1865	12.75	20.25	7.5

Source: Mary B. Rose, 'The Gregs of Styal . . .' (unpublished PhD thesis),
Appendix J.

Table 4.5 *Average stocks of raw cotton at Quarry Bank, 1858–67 (lb)*

	Raw cotton
1858	90,844
1859	250,500
1860	238,314
1861	283,790
1862	88,101
1863	51,534
1864	91,833
1865	78,150
1866	89,038
1867	76,582

Source: MCL C5/1/2/8, partnership accounts.

working. Nevertheless, production methods at the mill were efficient
enough for a respectable margin of profit to remain.

Greg's policy at Quarry Bank was, for the most part, cautious but
positive. By a combination of advance purchasing and contraction of
output he was able to reduce his purchases of the high-priced raw
materials considerably. Thus, from 1859 he began increasing his stocks
of raw cotton, as Table 4.5 shows. To conserve his stocks as far as was
possible he reduced output by short-time working, especially in 1862
and 1863. Yarn output was, therefore, more than halved in 1862–4
whilst cloth production was a little over one-third of its normal level,
as Table 4.6 shows.

Table 4.6 *Yarn and cloth production at Quarry Bank, 1858–67 (lb)*

	Yarn	Cloth
1858	974,950	932,863
1859	998,173	972,217
1860	988,538	946,705
1861	890,835	874,891
1862	404,100	391,195
1863	488,025	370,235
1864	532,240	363,219
1865	783,934	712,686
1866	898,094	827,888
1867	902,075	876,636

Source: MCL C5/1/7/1–2, spinning and weaving production accounts.

At the same time Greg began experimenting with cotton substitutes. Flax, jute and hemp, whilst of little use to the numerous fine yarn and cloth manufacturers, were attractive alternatives for the coarse producer. In August 1861 he told his eldest son '... I have found some flax growing in the garden will answer my purposes for the little experiment I wanted ... I have not yet got my samples to try fully our cotton machines, but as American now costs with waste and Surats 7d, there is room for doing something even now.'[28] He was not alone, and in the following year he wrote: 'Many substitutes for cotton are advertising and patenting and I am going into the city tomorrow to see two sorts, one from jute [is] promising but I have no doubt [it] will produce some change in our coarse manufacturers and possibly help to keep down the price by frightening the speculators and encouraging the trade by anticipating relief.'[29] The pursuit of a judicious sales policy meant that the firm avoided the worse effect of wartime uncertainty. Indeed, at Quarry Bank revenue only fell by 4.3% between 1861 and 1865.[30] In 1864 he outlined policies in the following terms to his son:

> ... I think a combination of circumstances may cause a further fall of 4d in cotton ... I should think that Reddish had better sell 12s and 18s than shut up at present price of cotton so long as they hold cotton to enable them to do so.
> I think Quarry Bank had better sell 12s and 14s twist and weft 12s, 14s and 17½ than stop so long at least as they hold cotton and by the time that is done we may see our way. We shall have plenty of failures large and small, but goods are scarce and some must buy them at such prices ...[31]

By displaying great care and understanding of the operation of volatile markets, Robert Hyde Greg, with the help of two of his sons, Edward and Henry, steered the two mills at Styal and Reddish through the hazards of the early 1860s. At Calver the picture was different. Since the product was similar to that spun at Reddish, it is reasonable to expect that the mill's fortunes would have been much the same. Differences in location and power supply, however, meant that the two mills had differing cost structures. Water power was used at Calver, whereas Reddish was steam-powered. Even before the American Civil War water mills were becoming less attractive. The benefit of water power had been that, despite high fixed costs, variable costs were low.[32] Reductions in the price of coal and improvements in the efficiency of steam, however, meant the erosion of this competitive advantage. In 1853, Robert Hyde Greg calculated '. . . now that coal is half the price and only 5 lb [per] horse power instead of 10 lb . . . the advantage of water power is reduced to ¼ of its former amount . . .'[33] This was not all. Increasingly during the 1840s and 1850s not only was the industry becoming more localised,[34] but commercial activity became centralised in Liverpool and Manchester. For the isolated rural mill like Calver, this substantially increased transport costs.

The American Civil War, which eroded fragile profits, saw the disappearance of many mills which, like Calver, were on the periphery of the industry. Indeed, it was in 1864 that John Greg sold his two mills at Lancaster and Caton to Storey Brothers. However, Calver's fortunes were unnecessarily damaged by incompetence. Henry Greg, whilst lacking the dynamism of a great businessman, ran Albert Mill very efficiently. As his father commented in 1856: 'Henry has made himself pretty well master of the thread business, quality and manufacture . . . we cannot do better than to let him look after all that concerns Reddish . . .'[35] Robert Philips Greg, however, was a totally inept businessman and his constant mismanagement of Calver and inability to maintain quality was a major factor in the mill's poor performance. At Quarry Bank, Edward's deficiencies were less apparent, since he worked in close contact with his father.

Robert Hyde Greg must, himself, take some of the blame for his eldest son's incapacity for, from childhood, he consistently sapped his confidence. Indulged by his mother, young Robert found his father exacting and unbending. Careless by nature, he had the very traits which most irritated his meticulous father. Even his schoolboy letters were scrutinised for poor handwriting. By adolescence, the position was so bad that they were barely speaking to each other and his mother tried to persuade her son to mend the broken relationship. She wrote:

. . . could you not dear son communicate with him a little more in conversation. If you knew how seriously and sorrowfully he says these things to me now and then you would take compassion on him and make an effort even if it were a great one. I know he feels deeply your want of communicativeness and though he pretends to laugh and joke it off, he rankles at his heart like a sore place.[36]

The consistently bad relationship with his father combined with an over-indulgent mother drained the young man of self-confidence and any potential competence. By the mid-1850s, Robert Hyde Greg was extending his biting criticism (with some justification) to his eldest son's management of Calver Mill and wrote in 1856 'You call me nervous and boast of your being a perfect financier. I kept strict accounts which you do not, and I know the incomings and accumulations where any and so forth and the responsibilities of my situation as a man of business.'[37] There can be little doubt that R. H. Greg and Company – and more especially Calver Mill – would have been better off without Robert Philips Greg. He had, however, little choice but to go into the firm and work with a man who consistently undermined him. Even after Calver was abandoned, he remained involved in marketing until 1871. By then, the position was intolerable and his decision to resign was greeted by relief tempered with scorn by his father, who wrote:

I have no doubt to become a country gentleman would on the whole conduce to your comfort and happiness more than remaining in business in Manchester. In the first place, I don't think your turn of mind and general character suitable for business either for comfort or success and it makes it difficult for your partners to act harmoniously as partners should do.[38]

Although Robert Hyde Greg was more tolerant towards his younger sons, they cannot have found him easy to work with. Like his father before him, he insisted on directing business policy until his retirement at 75. Samuel, however, whilst stubborn had been approachable; Robert was domineering and unbending. He drained much of the initiative from his sons, especially the older ones. Henry was a competent, but uninspired businessman. Only Arthur, the baby of the family – who never joined R. H. Greg and Company – was outstanding. He ultimately became chairman of Chadwick Brothers, the vast sewing cotton firm. His father's influence was only peripheral, whilst his position as the youngest meant he was probably treated more leniently than his brothers.

III Labour

Samuel Greg started creating a permanent labour force at Styal in the 1820s. It was, however, a slow process and until the 1840s labour of one sort or another continued to be imported to the village. The need, in 1834, for experienced operatives to go from Quarry Bank to assist in the opening of Lowerhouse Mill encouraged Robert Hyde Greg to import pauper labour from the South-East of England. Parish apprentices, on the other hand, continued to be used there, though in declining numbers, until 1847.

During the 1830s, Robert Hyde Greg and Edmund Ashworth (the Bolton cotton spinner), masterminded a campaign to persuade Edwin Chadwick, the Poor Law Commissioner, to make poor families from the South-East of England available to the millowners of the North. Angry that this had not been facilitated by the New Poor Law, he complained in September 1834 that 'At this moment our machinery in one mill has been standing for twelve months for hands. In another we cannot start our new machinery for the same want . . .'[39] The irony was, he argued, that whilst he and other manufacturers experienced a shortage of workers, there was a vast pool of surplus labour in the agricultural areas. Edmund Ashworth claimed that '. . . if an enterprising family ventured to leave their parish, they lose in the first place the pay they were receiving and, if on arrival in Lancashire or elsewhere they do not immediately meet with employment and are obliged to be on relief they are removed to their parish again, at its cost'.[40] Thus it was argued that by impeding mobility (except via emigration), Overseers encouraged a major waste of resources.

Edwin Chadwick was convinced of the expediency of a scheme whereby families could be moved from areas of labour surplus to those of dearth. The ensuing scheme was understandably unpopular, however, and between 1834 and 1836 only 329 families, comprising 2,673 individuals, migrated. They came from Norfolk, Suffolk, Berkshire, Buckinghamshire, Wiltshire, Hampshire, Oxfordshire, Bedfordshire, Essex, Cambridgeshire and Kent and moved to Lancashire, Cheshire and Derbyshire.[41] Depression, one of the most serious of the century, began in 1837 and the scheme likened by Oastler to 'transportation into slavery' was abandoned, never to be revived.

Robert Hyde Greg found the arrangement useful, and 30 individuals came to Styal from Great Bledlow, in Oxfordshire, in 1835. As was general under the scheme, a contract of employment was arranged, prior to the family's departure. They were housed in Styal and wages were calculated on a family basis under a two-year contract. As Table 4.7 shows, the family was employed in its entirety. The father, deemed to be too old to learn factory work, was generally employed on the farm, or as a general labourer around the mill. One family, named Worth, was hastily dismissed because '. . . the family turned out ill, having an ignorant, stupid mother'.[42] But, in general,

Table 4.7 *Wages paid in the first year to the Howlett family, who came to Styal in 1835*

	Per week (£ s d)		
John Howlett, aged 38 (employed at Oak Farm)		12	0
Mary Ann Howlett, aged 16		4	6
Ann Howlett, aged 14		3	6
Celia Howlett, aged 12		2	6
Timothy Howlett, aged 10		1	6
Total	1	4	0

Note: In the second year the family's income rose to 27s per week.
Source: MCL C5/1/13/2, wages book, 1835; *First annual report of the Poor Law commissioners* PP 1835 (500), xxxv p. 220.

Table 4.8 *Employment at Quarry Bank, 1816–50 (%)*

	Men	Women	Children
1816		30	70
1844	21	24	55
1848	30	36	34
1850	28	52	20

Source: Report on the state of children . . ., PP 1816 (397) III, p. 374; MCL C5/6/5, returns provided by R. H. Greg, 1844 and 1850; MCL C5/1/5/5, wages book 1848; MCL C5/4/3–4, age certificate book.

Greg was happy with the migrant workers, commenting that they were '. . . proper in their behaviour and diligent and tractable in their work'.[43] Housing was of reasonable standard in Styal and employment stable and regular. Additionally, wages were much higher. The family income of the Howletts, for instance, was the first year twice the level it had been in Oxfordshire.[44] As a result, most migrants stayed in Styal long after their two-year contracts had expired and became part of the permanent community. The Howletts, for example, still resided in Styal in 1861.[45] Of the Vearys, another southern family, Greg states: 'One son has become Master of the National School in an adjoining parish; one is a tailor, another a shoemaker. The conduct of this family has been uniformly respectable and their success correspondent.'[46] Labour from the agricultural south thus fulfilled a dual function, as far as Styal was concerned. It met short-term contingencies during the mid-1830s, but also became part of the permanent labour base.

The parish apprentices system was being run down at Styal during the 1830s and 1840s. Among the last employers to use parish children, the Gregs continued to find them convenient whilst large numbers of children were needed in the mill. Table 4.8 shows that it was not until the late 1840s that the proportion of children had declined to less than half the total. Several factors explain the decline in the use of child labour and subsequent demise of the parish apprentice system. As a result of what Greg described as 'Factory Bills, Short time Committees and Morbid Philanthropy' juveniles and pauper children in particular became less convenient. This undoubtedly encouraged him to alter his employment policies, rendering the parish apprentice system redundant at Styal. Expansion of activities to include weaving was crucial to the mill's survival in the 1840s. It had the added benefit of reducing the demand for children, since most jobs were done by women and young girls.

It remains to speculate on why pauper childen were used so much later at Quarry Bank than was general. After all, many employers claimed that apprenticed labour was 'in reality more expensive than paid labour and . . . troublesome inconvenient and objectionable in almost every point of view . . .'[47] The explanation would seem to be twofold. In the first place the Gregs had developed close links with the Liverpool poorhouse, which meant that large numbers of poor children were forthcoming. More important, however, was the exceptional nature of the water power. This was such that even after the Gregs had decided to create a permanent community, it was necessary to use apprentices as a supplement for many years.

The last child ended her term at Quarry Bank in 1847, almost twenty years after most firms had moved exclusively to free labour. This late use of pauper children did not go unnoticed. Pamphleteers, such as John Doherty, the Ten Hours Movement activist, were vociferous in their criticism. Angered by Robert Hyde Greg's opposition to a reduction in the working day, Doherty compared the condition of Styal apprentices unfavourbly with that of slaves on sugar plantations.[48]

By the 1840s, Styal had emerged as a substantial and stable community capable of supplying the needs of the mill, as Table 4.9 shows.

Throughout the mid-nineteenth century, the mill was the principal employer of the area; 40 per cent of the village population worked there. Although this declined so that, by 1871, slightly over 20 per cent of the village were mill hands, the factory still far outstripped other

Table 4.9 *The population of the village of Styal, 1787–1871*

	Males	Females	Total	Numbers employed at Quarry Bank
1787	n.a.	n.a.	420	n.a.
1841	374	490	864	435
1851	435	481	816	377
1861	393	409	802	321
1871	392	472	864	356

Sources: MCL C5/1/15/3–7, wages books; W. Lazenby, 'The economic and social history of Styal 1750–1850', (unpublished MA thesis, University of Manchester, 1949), p. 52; PRO HO 107/115, Census Enumerators' book for the township of Pownall Fee; CRO 1851–71, Census enumerators' books for the township of Pownall Fee.

occupations, such as agriculture and domestic service.[49] The absence of many alternatives in this area, combined with job security and a relatively high standard of comfort in Styal,[50] meant that the workforce at Quarry Bank remained fairly stable from the 1830s until the 1870s. With labour turnover averaging 15 per cent per annum between 1835 and 1866, Greg had achieved stability unparalleled in towns. Families, some of whom came to Styal in the 1820s, stayed in the village for generations. Names such as Sprowson, Penlington, Worthington, Henshall, Witney, Potts and Venables recur regularly in the wages books.[51]

IV Marketing

With the demise of the manufacturing partnership, it was only a matter of time before the brothers abandoned the Manchester firm. In 1844 the arrangement was terminated and Robert Hyde Greg took over sole control, renaming it R. H. Greg and Company. He was soon joined by his two sons, Robert and Henry. Robert Hyde Greg had two main objectives in his mercantile firm. He was keen to pursue a policy of safety and, at the same time, provide a good service for the Greg mills.

The memory of the losses which his father had incurred in overseas markets remained vivid with Robert Hyde Greg.[52] Keen to avoid similar problems, he instituted policies of risk aversion. By converting R. H. Greg and Company into a commission agency he transferred the burden of risk on to manufacturers – including the Greg mills. In

Thomas Venables and family

return for a commission, usually of 2½ per cent, to cover warehouse, transport and distribution costs, the firm sold yarn and cloth for manufacturers, often by private contract to meet specific orders. For a further commission, all bad debts were guaranteed. He was deeply suspicious of any suggestions from his sons to deviate from this policy and revert to the hazardous practice of shipping. In 1861 Robert Philips Greg tentatively embarked on such business and was rebuked by his father, who wrote that it was dangerous '. . . as you will find to your cost, as I found to the tune of thousands and your grandpapa to that of tens of thousands . . . I cannot by pen and voice explain and argue at full but you will find loss, vexation and interruption of financing of regular business . . .'[53] Nevertheless, from 1860 and more especially after 1865 when Robert Hyde Greg retired from the mercantile firm, risky shipments principally to China, Japan and India, the main areas of overseas growth for the cotton trade at this time, did occur.

In his approach to the American Civil War Robert Hyde Greg showed wisdom. A combination of caution and impeccable judgement guided the firm through a phase which witnessed the failure of merchants and manufacturers alike. By judicious stockpiling of yarn and goods – purchased on a non-commission basis at pre-1862 prices, as soon as there was a hint of war – he reaped healthy returns between 1862 and 1865, when yarn and cloth prices rose. He concentrated his activity largely on the home market, so that although he had speculated, he avoided the potential hazards of overseas uncertainty. His sons were, however, less fortunate after the war, though reductions in returns were not catastrophic.[54]

Robert Hyde Greg's principal concern, however, was to ensure that whilst the formal partnership was at an end, the marketing firm remained the servant of the Greg mills. He believed that by maintaining this role the firm would avoid the worst of the mistakes of his father's day. Thus, with the exception of the Bury mill sold in 1850, the constituent mills of the old conglomerate continued to sell their produce through the firm on a commission basis. The yarns of both Albert Mill, Reddish, and the Calver Mill were also sold in this way. So keen was he that the situation be maintained that when his sons suggested any deviation, he was stubborn in his opposition. In 1856, when Henry and Robert sought to extend the scope of the firm and increase the sales from other firms, he wrote:

Our concern there [Manchester] has always been and properly so, one for the disposal of the produce of our own mills though we have reasonably added a little commission and buying and selling of yarn and cotton. If we deviated from this we found we lost more by withdrawing our attention from our own concerns . . . I have always held out to our salesmen that GG [R. H. Greg and Company] was merely the servant of the mills, must accept their commands in all respects and if not would lose their business . . .[55]

His main worry about expanding the scope of their dealings was doubtless a valid one. He feared that by selling goods similar to those produced by Greg mills, their position might be undermined. This being so, these mills would possibly choose to conduct their own sales, even bankrupting the Manchester firm. Thus, he continued:

If we lose Bollington or Lancaster, it would perhaps break up our Manchester firm in its present form at least . . . The interests of Reddish are in no wise to be

Robert Hyde Greg aged 70

sacrificed to GG and, if they are, I hold that Reddish may cut the connection . . . GG must remember if it neglects our mills in introducing cheap goods, particularly under the character acquired by our mills, those mills both your uncles' and our own will . . . sell by salesmen of their own.[56]

It was in the London trade where doubled yarn and thread from Reddish was sold that he was most uneasy. He pointed out that it had taken '. . . a good time to establish and has been gained by furnishing an article constantly and regularly and to be depended upon and in this Reddish has had the merit wholly and not GG and ought to reap the chief advantage and GG ought not to try and supplant it with a cheaper article . . .'[57] This observation is espcaially pertinent, since it parallels the position of Quarry Bank yarns after the Napoleonic Wars. It highlights the capacity of the produce of individual mills to

Table 4.10 *Revenue and bad debts in R. H. Greg and Company 1857–74 (average per annum, £)*

	Com-mission	Profit on sales	Profit/loss on cotton dealing	Profit/loss on shipping	Bad debts
1857–9	4,594	1,721	—	—	165
1860–4	4,389	4,719	—	10 (loss)	198
1864–9	6,172	1,214	146 (loss)	38	1,815
1870–4	5,567	728	—	108 (loss)	319

Sources: MCL C5/1/2/8, partnership accounts; Greg brothers' accounts, 1865–1903.

command, through quality and regularity of delivery, a significant foothold in specific markets.

Robert Hyde Greg's 'safety first' policy, whilst hardly dynamic, proved successful, as Table 4.10 shows. As in manufacturing, he successfully piloted the firm through a hazardous and turbulent period.

V An assessment of Robert Hyde Greg

Robert Hyde Greg died on 21 October 1875. His main achievement was the preservation of his firm in a changing and turbulent economic climate. His success was, however, much less dramatic than his father's. Both started as wealthy men, heirs to considerable fortunes and the vast range of contacts which came with the business longevity. Samuel, however, greatly increased the size of his fortune, while Robert only maintained his. At £55,000 (excluding some land passed in trust to Robert Philips Greg), Robert Hyde Greg's estate was a fraction of his father's. Despite a lifetime of hard work, his business success was relatively limited. The explanation of the differing experience lies partly in circumstances and partly in personality. Profit margins were much higher during the industrial revolution than they became in the mid-nineteenth century. Samuel thus had greater capacity to diversify his investment and guarantee alternative income. As a result, all profits were retained in manufacturing, allowing expansion. Robert had some income from his land, but this was paltry compared with Samuel's. Consequently, he was forced to withdraw from his pool of profits in order to live.

It is, however, unlikely that even with the same opportunities Robert would have been as successful as his father. His was a more cautious nature and his investment policies lacked much of the imagination of his father. Not only this, but Samuel achieved his business success at the expense of most outside interests. Robert, on the other hand, was much less single-minded. His involvements included politics, experimental farming, mineralogy and genealogy. During the 1830s he was a committed and energetic member of the Anti-Corn Law League.[58] When he was interested in experimental farming, during the 1840s, he wrote three pamphlets: *Scottish farming in the Lothians* and *Scottish farming in England* were published in 1842, and *Improvements in agriculture* followed two years later. His painstaking and meticulous nature meant that he devoted excessive attention and energy to all his activities, which reduced the time he devoted to business. Even after he retired from politics, in 1846, his interests remained far wider than his father's had been.

Robert Hyde Greg did not, however, neglect his business, nor was he distracted by a quest for prestige. He became a substantial landowner more through inheritance than by design. Apart from the Styal Estate, which he bought in 1855 by selling land in Norfolk, most of his property was inherited either from his brother or his father. The Coles Estate, in Hertfordshire, became his in 1839 when his brother, Thomas, died. At the same time he was bequeathed the North American lands.[59] Under his father's will, along with his brothers, Robert received shares in the West Indies and Reddish estates. Interest in these led him, eventually, to buy out his brothers.[60] Robert, like his father, did not crave the prestige which came with land-owning. Any property was there to be worked and to generate income, or to be used as security for mortgage loans, which were then transferred into the cotton industry. The difference between them was that Samuel pursued a conscious investment policy, whilst Robert merely inherited. Robert owned more houses than his father, however, though neither Norcliffe Hall, Styal, nor Coles in Hertfordshire was extravagant. Norcliffe, like Quarry Bank House, was a necessity. Robert maintained that '[Quarry Bank Mill] . . . can be nothing unless I reside there more than any other mill, nor be of any interest to me'.[61] The house, which was neo-Elizabethan in style, was built as economically as possible. As he wrote to his father in 1829:

I am in hopes of getting cheaper off with building than I had expected . . . Johnson who gave me my elevation has been with me today, and on looking through my reduced plan and considering the price of things, he thinks he can come within £2,000 and is preparing an estimate and I have told him to cut down to that mark. If I can manage that I am sure I can live cheaper by £400 p.a. than I am now doing . . . I neither can nor will continue living at my present expense . . .[62]

Norcliffe Hall

His main luxury was his gardens. A keen horticulturist, he imported many exotic trees and shrubs to create magnificent displays at both Coles and Norcliffe. Nevertheless, only a tiny part of each estate was set aside for him to indulge his hobby.[63]

When he died Robert Hyde Greg was remembered with respect, rather than warmth. He was a diligent, meticulous old man for whom life may well have been a disappointment. His sons found him difficult to deal with, both at home and in business. The only people for whom he had any obvious affection were his wife, Mary, and his daughter, Caroline, who died when she was only 37 years old.

೫೩

The later Gregs, 1870–1914

For much of the nineteenth century it seemed that the British cotton industry could expand indefinitely; that ever-growing markets could swallow an infinite quantity of yarn and cotton. From 1873 onwards it became clear that this was an illusion and that the engine of growth had apparently lost its momentum. The spectre of foreign competition had long haunted industrialists but, in the 1870s, it became a reality. Tariffs were raised to protect infant industries in Britain's traditional markets and soon cottons faced competition in both foreign and home markets. Britain's near-monopoly abroad for manufactured goods was at last challenged. Despite efforts to shift to Empire and Far Eastern markets, pre-eminence in the world trade in cotton goods was lost for ever. Manufacturers faced a downward spiral in world prices which squeezed their profit margins and, ultimately, reduced demand for their products abroad.

Historians, struck by the apparent deterioration of Britain's position in the world economy and by the poor performance of the staple sectors, have cast around for an explanation. Time and again the economy's ills have been laid at the door of the entrepreneur. His lethargy and complacency, it has been argued, were responsible for the slow rate of innovation which made British goods uncompetitive.[1] It is a seductive theory, confirming popular prejudices, but one which collapses on close scrutiny. Doubtless, some industrialists lacked drive, but by no means all. The range of competence was infinite and most reacted rationally to a changing environment.[2]

The Gregs' fortunes varied considerably during the late nineteenth century. Edward Hyde Greg at Quarry Bank and his brother, Henry, at Reddish both encountered difficulties, especially during the 1880s. Edward, at Quarry Bank – locked into the production of coarse cloth in an antiquated mill – found himself in serious difficulties. Henry found survival easier at the more modern Albert Mill, and his son instituted a policy of specialisation, which proved a perfect response to a changed world. Reaction at the two mills varied, therefore, because of differences in production and location, as well as business competence. Such contrasting experience highlights the folly of assuming that the problems of the British cotton industry were the result of anything so simple as a deterioration in the quality of British entrepreneurship.

The sales partnership, renamed Greg Brothers, became more adventurous. The policy of offering an exclusive agency to the Greg mills was abandoned as too limiting. Instead, the firm became specialist commission agents, acting on behalf of a growing number of coarse producers. In an effort to diversify or perhaps to guarantee supplies of particular products they became directly involved in manufacturing. In an age of growing specialisation, this proved an unfortunate move, bringing only meagre and uncertain returns.

I Development and performance

Edward Hyde Greg took over Quarry Bank from his father in 1870. His thirty years as master were the most difficult in the mill's history. Faced with falling prices and profit margins, even the most competent and committed millowner would have had difficulties. Edward, with his many distractions, found the position intolerable.

Yarn and cloth prices in the cotton trade as a whole began to fall after the American Civil War – more a reaction to the inflated levels of the war years than to anything else. Had the downwards movement halted, there would have been few problems. It continued, however, almost uninterrupted for the next three decades, part of a world decline in prices. This downward spiral inevitably reduced profit margins, discouraging expansion and investment – especially in coarse production, which suffered most. Output consequently grew much more slowly than in earlier decades.[3]

The prosperity of the cotton industry had depended heavily on exports for much of the nineteenth century. Yet it was in foreign markets that the performance of the cotton industry was most disappointing. Yarn exports actually fell and cloth exports, which had been growing by 8.3 per cent per annum between 1820 and 1860, grew by a mere 1.4 per cent per annum between 1870 and 1910.[4] Britain's cotton manufacturers were, for the first time, facing foreign competition. The impact on demand was exacerbated by the effect of the world decline in prices, which reduced the import capabilities of many of Britain's customers.

Competition came first from the United States and a number of

Quarry Bank Mill from the weir

European countries, where cotton industries which had been developing from the 1830s grew rapidly. Initially, the threat was minimal.
Lancashire retained a comparative advantage in cotton production
and her merchants simply tapped new markets, such as India, the Far
East, South America and the Levant.[5] Matters deteriorated when tariff
protection was introduced in Europe and the United States, to protect
infant industries. Britain not only found many of her traditional
markets closed, she also began to face competition in her new
markets. India, Japan and China had all, in 1870, offered attractive
markets for Lancashire's yarn and cloth. By 1913, Japan had a thriving
cotton industry and was already challenging Britain in the yarn
markets of China and India. India, whilst remaining an important
market for cloth, became a significant producer and exporter of yarn

Table 5.1 *Quarry Bank Mill, 1870–1914*

	Numbers employed	Spindlage	Loomage	Output (lb) Yarn	Output (lb) Cloth	Percentage of total cloth output
1870	356	10,704	252	1,091,302	1,075,889	0.07
1880	299	9,543	284	752,812	731,452	0.07
1890	303	9,879	280	804,305	924,319	0.08
1900	192	–	406	–	1,122,986	0.09
1910	161	–	368 (+72)	–	1,011,410	0.09
1914	143	–	327 (+94)	–	790,129	0.05

Note: The numbers employed for 1870–90 are estimates based upon figures in the production accounts. These record only those directly employed in spinning and weaving. As a result, to reach the above totals, an allowance for other staff (based upon available wages books) has been made; the additional looms shown in brackets for 1910 and 1914 are Northrop looms. Total cloth output is a crude estimate, assuming that cloth output was 67% of total raw cotton consumption (derived from T. Ellison, *The Cotton Trade* ... p. 69).
Sources: B. Mitchell and P. Deane, *Abstract* ... , p. 179; T. Ellison, *The Cotton Trade* ... , p. 69; MCL C5/1/7/3, spinning and weaving production accounts; MCL C5/1/15/10–11, wages books.

within Asia.[6] Not only was there competition in foreign markets, but the United Kingdom began to import some cotton yarn and goods. These imports increased eightfold between 1870 and 1913.[7] The effect of the international growth of the cotton industry was that Britain's share of world trade in cotton textiles declined. In the years 1882–4 the British cotton industry's share of world trade in cotton goods was 82 per cent; by 1910 to 1913, it had declined to 58 per cent.[8]

At Quarry Bank the most remarkable features of the late nineteenth century, as Table 5.1 shows, were the shrinkage of the workforce, the ending of spinning in 1894 and the continued erosion of the mill's position in terms of national cloth output.

At first all went well at Styal. The only major disruption in the early 1870s was a serious flood in one of the weaving sheds. On 18 June 1872:

A terrific storm broke over the parish ... lasting till midnight. During the night, the rush of water down the Bollin (increased by the bursting of the bank of the Macclesfield Canal at Bollington) was such to flood the dwellings in the lower part of the village of Bollington. At Messrs Gregs' mill at Quarry Bank, Styal, the lower room was submerged and considerable damage done ...[9]

Inevitably, production in the affected weaving shed was disrupted and 103 hours' output was lost. The overall impact on production that

Table 5.2 *The profit surplus at Quarry Bank, 1870–1902*

	Average per annum (£)
1870–4	+3,440
1875–9	+ 993
1880–4	− 824
1885–9	− 788
1890–4	− 555
1895–9	− 906
1900–2	+ 30

Source: Quarry Bank memoranda, 1784–1850 (profit surplus shown in notes at the back).

year was, however, minimal. As soon as repairs were completed the lost time was recovered at the rate of five hours per week, until December. The first half of the 1870s were, therefore, fairly prosperous, with profits averaging £3,440 per annum, as Table 5.2 shows.

Quarry Bank was, however, especially badly affected during the series of slumps of the late nineteenth century. An old rural mill producing coarse yarns and cloth, it was particularly vulnerable to the ravages of foreign competition. Orders and sales declined and short-time working became normal. By 1879, sales had sunk to £29,401 a year – a fall of 45.6% on the average for the first half of the decade. Further deterioration followed, and during the late 1880s sales were a mere £28,000 a year.[10] The combination of falling prices and the short-time working, which increased unit costs, proved disastrous for profits. Soon, the mill was running at a loss which averaged £768 a year from 1880 to 1899.[11]

The prospects were bleak and Edward feared that the mill would fail. In 1887, he complained to his cousin, George Melly, 'I fear Quarry Bank Mill is on its last legs. Never since I commenced have things looked so black and hopeless. Not only ruinous loss on sales but no sales and orders at all.'[12]

The following year he was even more despondent when he concluded 'Our cotton business [is] as bad as ever. The ten years previous to the devaluation of silver [1873] Quarry Bank made thousands a year. The ten years after it averaged a thousand a year loss. I work harder than ever before, and for what for always loss, loss, loss.'[13] Edward did attempt to restore the mill's fortunes. Between 1888 and 1892 he spent £1,034 on installing ring spinning frames. During a period when entrepreneurs have been criticised for their inertia in the

Table 5.3 *Yarn output per man/hour at Quarry Bank, 1880–94*

	Yarn output per man/hour (lb)
1880	2.43
1885	2.54
1890	2.33
1894	2.61

Source: MCL C5/1/7/2–3, spinning and weaving production books.

face of new technology,[14] Edward appears far-sighted. Too much should not be made of his decision, however. Ring frames, whilst arguably inefficient for the fine Lancashire industry,[15] were potentially suitable for Styal with its coarse output: the effect on the mill's fortunes, however, was strictly marginal since their impact on productivity at Styal seems inconclusive, as Table 5.3 shows. Spinning was finally abandoned at Quarry Bank in 1894, leading many families to leave Styal. By concentrating solely on weaving, Greg hoped for better returns, in a world of growing specialisation.

Edward Hyde Greg was an enigma. Extravagant, vain and eccentric, he none the less left a fortune of over £85,000.[16] He showed little commitment to Quarry Bank and his attempts to live the life of the squire not only drained the mill, but led the Norcliffe Estate (inherited from his father) to be mortgaged and ultimately let, to raise money. Happy to buy steam yachts whilst his mill foundered, he withdrew over £2,000 per annum from Quarry Bank, from 1871 to 1890.[17] Even his sons commented on his extravagance and Edward Hyde Jr wrote in 1884:

... I am very sorry to hear such very dismal reports but I really think you are most inconsistent. In one and the same breath ... you talk of utter bankruptcy and giving dinner parties and getting me gold solitaires ... Why are you giving a dinner party? What right have you to give one if you are as you say on the very verge of bankruptcy and if you are not why do you write the dismal letters to me and others ... I don't even remember having a cheerful letter from you in six years.

Here is a beginning which I have suggested several times only you never will do anything (1) Cease to keep Ally and Jack at expensive schools where they are doing no good and learning nothing and costing £300 a year for this edifying occupation, (2) Ernest has just had his salary raised to £200 a year so drop his allowance entirely. We mustn't expect any longer to be able to dress as we used to and get as good articles as we used to and we must abandon this notion that we have got a position to keep up. We cannot do it and we mustn't try. I cannot understand where all the money went to when we were

Edward Hyde Greg

prosperous, not a penny ever seems to have been put by, and yet what have
we got to show for all this expenditure. Hunters, Traps? Dog Carts?
Carriages? Nothing all gone in fritter, now when we want money not a
penny . . .'[18]

Not only was Edward Hyde Greg extravagant, he was incurably vain
and was repeatedly photographed in various military and ceremonial
guises. It seems that he may almost have seen Quarry Bank as an

Quarry Bank mechanics, c. 1892

Repairs to mill dam, *c.* 1900

unfortunate accident of birth which he was relieved to pass on to his son, Robert Alexander, in 1900.

Economic prospects were more favourable in the new century. A full programme of modernisation was started in an attempt to revitalise the mill. The first priority was to update the power supply. It had long been recognised that the high cost of bringing coal to Styal made

Table 5.4 *Cloth output per man/hour at Quarry Bank, 1885–1914*

	Cloth output per man/hour (lb)
1885	2.37
1890	2.32
1895	2.02
1900	2.31
1905	2.79
1910	2.60
1914	2.94

Source: MCL C5/1/7/2–3, spinning and weaving production books.

steam power uneconomic as a principal source; other variations were, however, feasible. In 1903 despite major repairs the massive water wheel, which had been in use for 80 years, was scrapped. The small supplementary steam engine was also removed. They were replaced by a modern 220-horse-power water turbine system, which was completed in 1904.[19]

Of primary concern, however, were measures which could significantly increase competitiveness and save the mill, without which the village of Styal could not have survived. In 1894 the automatic Northrop loom was introduced in America.[20] It diffused very slowly in Britain, indeed by 1914 only 1 or 2 per cent of looms were Northrops in Britain as compared with 40 per cent in the United States.[21] Although some historians have used this as still further evidence of technological inertia, it has been shown that the Northrop was unsuitable for the Lancashire product and inappropriate where labour was relatively plentiful.[22] In 1909 Robert Alexander Greg introduced Northrops to Quarry Bank and by 1914 there were 94.[23]

That the automatic loom was introduced so early at Quarry Bank was the result of several factors. In the first place, Henry Philips Greg was instrumental in importing the first Northrops to Britain in 1902.[24] Doubtless he encouraged his cousin to experiment with the looms in an effort to save the ailing mill by reducing costs. Most jobs at Quarry Bank were, by 1900, carried out by women and young girls and alternative employment in the area was scarce. Thus many families left the area, quite apart from those who left on the abandonment of spinning. As a result, labour was becoming relatively scarce in Styal, encouraging the adoption of a labour-saving device such as the Northrop. Fortuitously, the looms were especially suitable for the

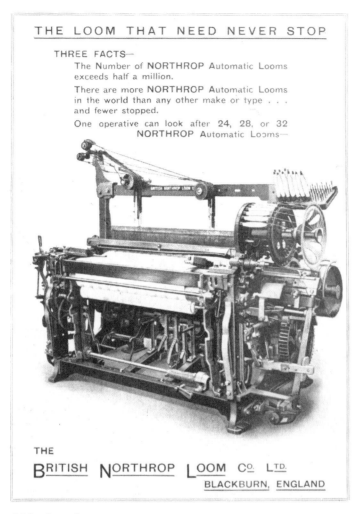

THE LOOM THAT NEED NEVER STOP

THREE FACTS—

The Number of NORTHROP Automatic Looms
exceeds half a million.

There are more NORTHROP Automatic Looms
in the world than any other make or type . . .
and fewer stopped.

One operative can look after 24, 28, or 32
NORTHROP Automatic Looms—

THE

BRITISH NORTHROP LOOM CO. LTD.
BLACKBURN, ENGLAND

A Northrop loom

coarse cloth produced at Styal. Unlike ring frames, which seem to
have had only a marginal impact on efficiency there, Northrops
increased productivity. As Table 5.4 shows, after a period of stag-
nation in the late nineteenth century, output per man/hour improved
after 1910. Unfortunately, it is not possible to determine what effect
this had on profitability. Research suggests that at their mills at Hyde,
the Ashtons did not enjoy substantial savings as a result of introducing Northrops.[25] At Styal, however, the picture was more favourable,

labour costs per lb on Northrops were 0.3d as compared with 0.9d on plain looms. This was principally the result of increasing the number of looms to 19 per man (for automatics) by 1914, as compared with only 6 plain looms. This was a much higher work-load than the Ashtons achieved. Inevitably, the innovation reduced the size of the workforce at Quarry Bank, hastening the further exodus of families from Styal. Without it, however, the mill's closure would have been speeded up, causing much greater unemployment.

In explaining why Northrops were adopted slowly in Lancashire, Sandberg had argued that not only were entrepreneurs acting rationally in view of their particular product, but that they faced substantial trade union opposition. This was especially true of the Ashtons, who encountered two much publicised strikes in 1906 and 1908.[26] Subsequently, however, this idea has been challenged by the suggestion that union opposition was more the result of Ashton's policies than of new technology.[27] Just what the attitude of the workforce at Styal was is unclear. There were two weavers' strikes – each of four months' duration – in 1907 and 1908. It is possible that these were to register opposition to any proposal to introduce Northrops. The evidence is, however, inconclusive, and their operation after 1909 seems to have been trouble-free.[28]

There were also difficulties at Albert Mill during the late nineteenth century. In 1876, Henry Russell Greg complained 'At Reddish we have a sad lack of orders. The Russian and Levant markets are so bad . . . '[29] By 1890, matters had become so serious that he stated: '£14 is more than I can make out of the mill in four years with £40,000 of capital . . . '[30]

More modern, larger and more specialised than Quarry Bank, Albert Mill was, however, an altogether more promising proposition. It fell to Henry Philips Greg, Henry Russell's son, to inject new life into the mill. In 1887, at the age of 22 Henry Philips began work with his father, as an office boy. By progressing through all branches, both clerical and manufacturing, he gained a deep understanding of the mill and the duties of its 400 employees. When his father died in 1894 he was well equipped to take control. Almost immediately, he began a programme of expansion and specialisation which was to secure the mill's success for decades to come. Emphasis was shifted to the production of fancy yarn for use in upholstery fabrics. Old machinery was scrapped and ring spindles installed. In 1907, a new two-storey mill was added. By the winter of 1913–14 fancy yarns became so important that a new building, specifically for fancy doubling, was added.

Table 5.5 *Income to Greg Brothers, 1870–99 (£)*

	Commission	Profit on sales	Profit/loss on shipments
1870–4	4,948	1,006	108 (loss)
1875–9	6,679	1,680	270 (loss)
1880–4	7,561	2,226	12 (loss)
1885–9	7,426	2,265	—
1890–4	6,690	3,019	16
1895–9	6,003	2,064	14

Source: Greg Brothers accounts, 1865–1903 (in possession of Mr W. Salt of Styal).

A deep understanding of the changing competitive environment inspired Henry Philips Greg to move into fancy yarns in the late nineteenth century. Traditional markets, even for doubled yarns, were becoming flooded, as competition – especially from abroad – increased. Specialisation, whilst risky, could provide an ideal choice. Demand for ready-made, upholstered furniture soared in the years before and after World War I, aided by the rise of department stores. An early lead in fancy yarns gave Greg a reputation for high quality and reliability, and for a while he enjoyed a near-monopoly.[31]

Of all the Gregs after Samuel, Henry Philips was perhaps the most talented, and for many years was at the forefront of the cotton industry. Dynamic and possessing unusual foresight, he realised the fundamental importance of research and new technology for the survival of his industry. In addition to numerous directorships, it has been mentioned that he was the chairman of the British Northrop Loom Company and was instrumental in the first importation of these looms from the United States in 1902. He was also deeply involved in the formation of the British Cotton Association and the establishment of the research laboratories at the Shirley Institute in Didsbury, Manchester.[32]

II Marketing

Sales of Greg yarn and cloth had always been via their marketing partnership in Manchester. This firm had, throughout, generally subordinated all other business. Output from the Greg mills, however, declined as mills were sold or became uncompetitive and a change of policy became imperative. Greg Brothers (as the firm was called after Robert Hyde Greg's retirement) began to expand its commission work, concentrating on the coarse yarns and cloth in which they were so experienced; the firm became agent for a growing range of spinners and weavers. By 1884, six spinners, four combined mills and two weavers (including the Gregs themselves) sold their products through the firm.[33] Greg Brothers, careful to protect the interests of the family's mills, ensured that the products of the independent firms, whilst coarse, were finer than those produced by the Gregs.

Commission was their main source of income in the late nineteenth century, as Table 5.5 shows. They did, however, do some dealing (shown as 'Profit on sales') in yarn and cloth and made a few foreign shipments. They were far more successful as dealers, selling yarn and cloth to Manchester merchants, than they were in their foreign shipments. Uncertainty and imperfect knowledge of overseas market conditions made direct foreign business hazardous. Between 1875 and 1881, net losses on shipments to Japan totalled £1,410. This was, however, counter-balanced by commission and profits on home sales, so that returns in Greg Brothers averaged 10.4 per cent per annum between 1870 and 1899.[34] It was unfortunate, not to say inexplicable at a time of difficulty in manufacturing, that this highly successful mercantile firm was tempted to diversify. Their two sorties into manufacturing were far from profitable. During the 1870s and 1880s, they bought a spinning and doubling mill in Stockport and acted as managing directors at Cressbrook Mill in Derbyshire. Dull market conditions meant it was the worst possible time to be involved in mill-owning, especially when the mills concerned were old, comparatively small and, where Cressbrook was concerned, isolated. Poor day-to-day management, combined with lack of direct supervision by Greg Brothers, aggravated the situation, and the experiments were failures.[35]

III Assessment of the later Gregs

The business environment in the late nineteenth century was exceptionally challenging. For the Gregs, long establishment, especially at Quarry Bank, had created its own obsolescence. Edward Hyde Greg's attitude and general eccentricity did not help matters. At the newer Albert Mill, radical modernisation sowed the seeds of future prosperity. In viewing the later Gregs it is interesting to consider the 'third generation thesis'. Struck by the apparent decline of and inadequate innovation in manufacturing, many historians looked for their explanations among the late Victorian entrepeneurs. Complacency, many believed, made businessmen's response to competition half-hearted, particularly when their families had been in business for generations. In such circumstances, other distractions, such as landowning and 'playing the country gentleman' are said to have reduced vigour.[36]

Such a theory is doubtless seductive. Yet, as an explanation of entrepreneurial failure (if there was any), it is questionable. In the first place, given the high failure rate of firms during the nineteenth century, it seems that comparatively few businessmen came from later generations of business families. Moreover, from this case it is clear that any generalisation concerning the incompetence of later generations is grossly misleading.

🖾🖾

CHAPTER 6

Paternalism and labour management

Satisfactory industrial relations were as crucial to business success during the industrial revolution as they are today. Entrepreneurs then as now were keen to ensure that productivity was high so that they could enjoy maximum returns. Absenteeism, lateness, sickness, carelessness, rapid labour turnover and strikes all harm profitability, and ways of reducing and preventing them remain at the heart of labour management.

During the industrial revolution efficiency was stimulated in a variety of ways. These ranged from the overtly coercive to the persuasive. Ironically it was the pioneers who, faced with creating the first factory labour force, had the most effective tool at their disposal – that of paternalism. The relationship between rich and poor in pre-industrial England was broadly paternalistic.[1] The basis of this was the notion that wealth carried with it certain obligations, including attending to the needs of subordinates, especially the poor. The rich were thus 'in loco parentis, guiding and restraining them like children'.[2] The poor, as dependants, owed their benefactors loyalty and obedience. In this way, the divisions of a hierarchical society could be maintained. Many manufacturers during the early phases of industrialisation applied this philosophy.[3] Paternalism was both a popular and a reasonably effective policy amongst rural millowners. The isolated factory colonies were an ideal environment for a close dependent relationship to develop between employer and employed. The so-called model factory owners like Owen, the Gregs, the Ashtons and the Ashworths were merely exploiting this capability. By contrast, their successors in towns were rarely community builders. Thus, whilst some of them recognised the potential fruits of paternalism, their half-hearted efforts had little real effect. In the late nineteenth century, a few employers such as Lever, Rowntree and Cadbury incorporated paternalism into their schemes for scientific management, adding training schemes and high wage policies to the traditional arsenal of model villages, recreational facilities and libraries.[4]

The policies of rural manufacturers should be seen in the context of the eighteenth and early nineteenth centuries. To modern Western eyes they seem unduly restrictive, if not intrusive. They undoubtedly enabled employers to exercise a high degree of control over their workforce. Yet in an age without a welfare state, the activities of these largely benevolent despots had benefit for their employees. Sick Clubs, decent living conditions, wholesome food, libraries and, most important, job security, were all enjoyed by many rural factory workers. The price was sometimes, though not invariably, political freedom. Yet, for many, if the alternative was living in uncertainty and urban squalor, it was a freedom they were rightly or wrongly prepared to forgo. There are modern parallels. In Japan, for example, overtly paternalistic policies in large-scale companies are the norm and are highly successful. Total loyalty is expected from all workers. In return, all their needs – including housing, welfare and leisure activities – are provided by the firm.[5]

For over 150 years the Gregs were paternalistic employers. Their policies at both Styal and Reddish were successful in creating a high degree of efficiency and industrial harmony. In return for good living and working conditions, they expected hard work and commitment. They were successful because their welfare and educational schemes were an integral part of business policy. At Bollington, Samuel Greg Jr tried to conduct a social experiment. This proved to be a fundamental error since, in so doing, he neglected his business and thus threatened the very security and harmony he sought to create.

I The development of factory colonies

The development of a factory colony was an essential part of investment for the rural millowner. By providing chapels, schools, shops, churches and recreational facilities, in addition to houses, he was not only creating a pleasant environment for his workers, but also tightening the links with the workforce. Industrial paternalists believed that if they enriched the lives of their operatives they would be rewarded by a more efficient factory. This was because ' . . . they [the workers] mostly understood that the master's interest is their own'[6] and they would thus work harder. Moreover, the high degree of control each employer exercised could prevent unwelcome developments, like drunkenness and labour unrest.

In practice, there were several ways in which factory colonies could create efficiency in rural mills. In the first place, housing, whilst fairly simple, tended to be clean and well constructed, most cottages having gardens. A labour force living in comfortable surroundings, with plenty of fresh food, was likely to be healthy. Days lost through sickness were thus kept to a minimum. Schools, chapels and evening classes not only provided basic education but were frequently used to teach the middle-class values of hard work and sobriety. Henry Ashworth, for example 'always [preferred] a child who has been educated at an infant school as those children are obedient and docile . . .'[7] Most rural millowners lived close to their factories and generally owned the land on which the village was built. This not only increased the sense of community interdependence, but also meant they could supervise all activities closely and restrict any they felt were undesirable. Drunkenness could cause many working days to be lost. Some, like Arkwright,[8] recognised that controlled drinking need not be damaging. Many, however, of the mainly Nonconformist factory masters banned drinking and beerhouses in their villages. They hoped other interests and recreations would prove an adequate diversion. Whilst operatives in rural communities may have had little freedom, they often enjoyed job security – a rare privilege in an age of uncertainty.

Factory colonies may possibly have increased diligence and regularity of work, but most employers found that overall productivity could be improved by schemes of punishments or incentives within the mill. Most popular were fines for shoddy workmanship. Piece rates, on the other hand, provided their own discipline. More enlightened employers, such as Strutt, experimented with bonus schemes, whilst Owen used what he described as a 'silent monitor'. This was a coloured piece of wood which hung beside each machine to denote the operative's behaviour during the previous day.[9]

Factory colonies varied in size from the relatively modest affairs of North Lancashire to extensive developments like Cromford, Belper and Hyde. Saltaire in the West Riding remains, however, the ultimate industrial community. Expenditure totalling £129,552 was made on 850 stone dwellings, a church and a school.[10] Others were more modest and depended on the scale of the mill and the scope of development. Even where only housing was provided, £50–£150 for a cottage for seven to ten people was normal. Predictably, it was the more substantial industrialists who could afford to be the most energetic paternalists. Thus, their employees were offered the widest range of facilities. As W. C. Taylor pointed out ' . . . great capitalists are more equitable and merciful employers than persons of limited fortune . . .'[11]

It is difficult to calculate the impact of paternalism on efficiency in rural mills. Robert Owen was, however, convinced that returns were commensurate with the level of investment. In 1813 he wrote ' . . . from experience which cannot deceive me I venture to assure you that your time and money so applied, if directed by a true knowledge of the subject would return you not 5, 10 or 15% for your capital so expended but often 50 and in many cases 100%'.[12] Although perhaps exaggerating the potential benefits of paternalism, Owen does illustrate that such policies could prove successful management tools. His view was echoed a century later by Cadbury, who wrote 'The supreme principle [behind Bournville] has been the belief that business efficiency and the welfare of employees are but different sides of the same problem.'[13]

Paternalism was not only successful in creating general mill efficiency, it would also prove a highly effective method of controlling trade unions. In the first place, the very isolation of many factory colonies meant that most rural millworkers rarely came into contact with trade unions or even their literature. Manufacturers hoped, too, that loyalty would prevent operatives from joining combinations. In any case, the rural employers had the ultimate weapon – the threat of loss of job, home and security. This almost certainly discouraged many from joining trade unions and helped to create industrial harmony. Urban factory masters, however, were bereft of any effective response to mass labour unrest. As more and more mills were steam-powered in the 1820s and 1830s, a growing proportion were in towns, where mill masters had no need to be community builders. Thus, their relationship with their operatives was impersonal. Added to this, the widespread use of dismissal as a disciplinary tool during depressions created an atmosphere of distrust. As a result the tumult of the late 1830s, which culminated in the Plug Riots of 1842, affected them far more severely than it did the 'model' manufacturers. It is interesting that, subsequently, a few became half-hearted paternalists. They provided tea parties and organised day trips, in the fond hope that it would stem the spread of trade unions and protect them from strikes. Had these moves been accompanied by the provision of housing or had there been a readiness to offer greater job security or make concessions on wages, they might have succeeded. As it was, most operatives remained justifiably cynical.[14]

II Styal: the management of apprentices

Styal offered ample opportunities for paternalistic management and, throughout its history, the Gregs pursued these policies. In the early

The Apprentice House

years, Samuel Greg's humanitarian treatment of his apprentices was almost certainly designed to encourage them to work and to discourage truancy. It was, however, in the 1820s, when he and his son set about creating a permanent workforce,[15] that his labour policies had a lasting effect. He created a stable community where labour turnover and unrest were at a minimum. Robert Hyde Greg, although unpopular with working-class activists, maintained this tradition, as did his successors.

By no means sentimental about their parish children, the Gregs none the less treated them well, by the standards of the time. Theirs was a classic paternalistic stance, as Robert Hyde Greg showed when he wrote:

... when there is no natural guardian ... the law transfers to a master the privileges of a parent among which is a command over the services of the child. It most properly imposes upon him also the duties of a parent, the providing of food, clothing and education of the child as far as it can enforce the same, it ought to impose the duty of humanity and kind treatment ... [16]

All surviving accounts suggest that these aims were fulfilled. The Apprentice House was, according to one ex-apprentice, comfortable '... the rooms were very clean, the floors frequently washed, the

Table 6.1 *Weekly expenses per apprentice at Quarry Bank in 1842*

	s	d	
Food	3	6¼	
Clothing		10¼	
Lodging		10¾	
Other	1	2	
Total	6	5¼	

Source: C5/1/7/2, apprentices' expenses.

rooms aired every day and white washed once a year. Our beds were good, we slept two to a bed and had clean sheets once a month, new clothes for Sundays once in two years and new working jackets when those had worn out.'[17] There was always plenty of locally produced fresh food. Vegetables from the Apprentice House garden and meat and cheese from Oak Farm added variety to a diet of milk, bread, potatoes and porridge.[18] When apprentices were ill they were treated by Mr Holland, who was the Styal Medical Officer for more than forty years. His primary function was to check that new apprentices were fit, but he also treated them later on when, for example, their eyes became inflamed owing to cotton dust – a common ailment. Styal apprentices received a fairly broad education, unlike New Lanark pauper children in David Dale's time, who were taught only 'such branches of education as were deemed to be useful to children of their situation'.[19] The three Rs and religious instruction were a matter of course, but their education went much further. Even the earliest recruits to Styal were taught music[20] and the girls were taught to sew. They competed for annual prizes presented at Christmas. Henry Russell Greg remembered the Apprentice Night with pleasure, ' . . . when we boys sat on top of boxes to be given to the departing apprentices – the table with rows of prizes, the coffee cans and the buns and Mrs Shawcross's private pantry . . .'[21] The Styal apprentices almost certainly owed their liberal schooling to Mrs Hannah Greg. Her Unitarian upbringing taught her the value of education for all. Whether or not the young factory apprentices appreciated her efforts after 12 hours of work is doubtful.

Inevitably, there was a cost attached to such paternalism – the weekly expenditure it involved. This varied with the number of children, since some costs, such as the salary of the Apprentice House Superintendent or the schoolmaster, were overheads. In December 1834 there were 80 apprentices costing 4s 0d each per week;[22] by 1842,

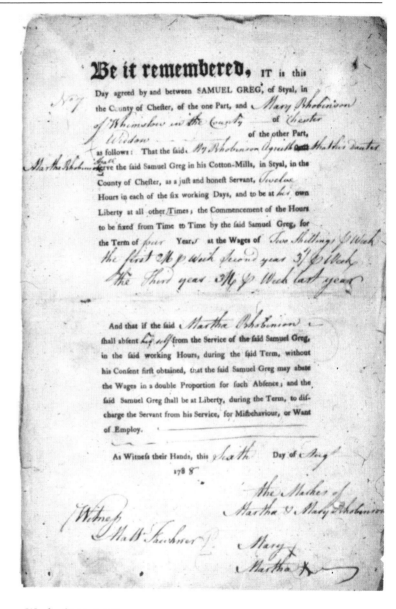

Worker's contract

when only 52 were employed, the weekly cost had risen to 6s 5¼d, as Table 6.1 shows. Until 1836 the Apprentice House was superintended by Mr George Shawcross and his wife, for a salary of £10 per year. Following Shawcross's death the job was taken by John Timperley, at an annual salary of £20. He stayed only until 1841, to be replaced by George Henshall.[23] Whilst apprentices were clearly more expensive than free children who, in the 1840s, earned around 5s 0d per week, it was economic to employ this type of labour and treat it well. It has been shown that it is unlikely that sufficient alternative labour would have been forthcoming.[24] Moreover, apprentice labour could provide the paternalist with the opportunity to experiment. By treating it well, he might be rewarded with greater efficiency; thus the costs of parish apprenticeship might yield a return. So, although a degree of humanity lay behind Samuel Greg's good treatment of his apprentices, it was also business sense.

Hours were long and the work in the early cotton mills hard; thus only healthy children survived and worked efficiently. Varied diet and a clean, airy apprentice house ensured strong apprentices. As a result there were comparatively few deaths at Quarry Bank, and hardly any were the result of mill work.

Truancy among parish apprentices bedevilled most cotton masters, disrupting work in their mills. By making his parish children comfortable, Greg hoped to discourage them from running away. Children far from home, unused to discipline, even in relatively comfortable surroundings, will run away occasionally, however. Although Greg suffered less from truancy than some of his contemporaries, he did not entirely prevent it.[25] It was rare for children to run away simply because they hated Quarry Bank. Some, like Thomas Priestley and Joseph Sefton, had no complaint against Greg, they simply wanted to see their families. One or two, such as William Tittenson, ran away to become soldiers. Some, however, were regular truants – difficult children, the product of extreme urban poverty. Truancy caused sufficient inconvenience to merit fairly severe punishment. Runaway apprentices, who were caught, repaid the cost of returning by working overtime. Regular offenders, however, were dealt with more strictly. In 1802, for example, John Wright, William Wright and Edward Tittenson were sentenced to between fourteen days' and one month's detention in Middlewich House of Correction for running away. This did not deter John Wright, who was so troublesome that he was finally dismissed, in 1809, because he had:

...as an apprentice frequently misbehaved himself and particularly hath often run away and left his said apprenticeship and in other respects very much misbehaved himself and we having duly examined into the truth of the complaint and the allegations of the partners, it manifestly appears to us that the said John Wright is guilty of the several charges made against him, we hereby discharge the said John Wright from Samuel Greg and Peter Ewart.[26]

It was his attitude to truancy which led Robert Hyde Greg into conflict with the Manchester Short Time Committee. In 1836 Esther Price and another apprentice, Lucy Garner, ran away during Wilmslow Wakes Week, not returning for several days. Not long before this incident Greg had ruled that any apprentice who ran away should have her hair cut off. Fortunately for the two girls, Robert's sister persuaded him that this was unnecessarily harsh, not to say degrading. Thus, he consulted a local magistrate who suggested that solitary confinement in a room in the Apprentice House would be appropriate. Consequently, the girl was imprisoned with '. . . the windows . . . boarded, partly to prevent communication from without, partly to prevent her escape. The room was . . . dark. Her food milk, porridge and bread morning and evening was the same as the other girls.'[27] By Greg's testimony, Esther Price had long been troublesome. Nevertheless, the punishment seems unusually severe. It came to light when some of her relatives contacted both the Liverpool Overseers (who had apprenticed her) and the Short Time Committee – a group of working-class activists. If nothing else, this incident shows that whilst Greg was prepared to guarantee good working conditions, he expected complete obedience in return.

The long hours of work, followed by school, deliberately left little time for mischief. Nevertheless, like all children they found some. Stealing apples and throwing stones, both normal childhood pranks, obviously annoyed Greg and his neighbours. No amount of good food and kind treatment was likely to prevent it. Quite big fines, such as five shillings for stealing apples, were imposed and met by working overtime. This punishment served the dual purpose of keeping the child out of further mischief and ensuring that extra jobs were done in the mill. Paternalism was thus moderately successful in encouraging the Styal apprentices to work hard and efficiently. The children were healthy and so were able to work consistently. Although there was some truancy, it is likely that it would have been much higher, had conditions at the mill been bad.

It was, however, in the creation of a stable community with minimal labour unrest that the Greg's management policies really succeeded – helped, of course, by the mill's isolated position. Until the 1820s, Samuel Greg had little interest in large-scale community development. From then on he set out to make the mill and the village

IN THE VILLAGE, STYAL

Styal village

self-contained. It proved relatively easy to encourage his ex-apprentices to stay; this was further proof that paternalism could prove successful. Similarly his son attracted operatives by offering them cottages and giving them the necessary incentives to stay.[28]

III Styal: paternalism and the factory colony

For a mill such as Quarry Bank to be developed, it was essential for housing to be provided. The cost was high. Before 1815 around £1,000 was spent on cottages and a further £300 on the Apprentice House.[29] It was, however, between 1819 and 1831 that the major expenditure took place. Over £6,000 was spent on cottage development: this was nearly 18 per cent of the total required to expand Quarry Bank. This included 42 cottages and a manager's house.[30] Later on, Robert Hyde Greg built more new cottages. In the last ten years of his life alone, he spent £2,838 on accommodation, quite apart from normal repairs. He built ten new cottages and a new road and renovated four existing properties.[31] By 1873 he owned 108 cottages, housing 538 people. By following the lead of Arkwright, Strutt and Owen and providing far more than just housing, the Gregs ensured that this investment was remunerative.

Oak Cottages, showing allotments

The cottages at Styal were little different in size from any other factory housing. There were, however, no 'back-to-backs' and this, combined with the absence of overcrowding and the provision of a separate privy for each cottage, made them vastly superior to urban working-class dwellings. The best cottages in Styal had '. . . a parlour and a back kitchen and two bedrooms, a cistern and a yard'.[32]

The Oak Cottages also had cellars, intended for hand-looms,

Styal co-operative store, village shop from 1823

though after power looms were added at Quarry Bank in the 1830s, many families took a lodger in these basement rooms. Unlike cottages in towns, where ten people commonly lived in one room, these cottages housed seven or eight people.[33] Each family had a good-sized garden; indeed during the nineteenth century the Oak Cottages all had a long strip of land, extending over what is now the village green. Styal operatives could thus grow their own vegetables. At the same time, because it was a country district, there was a plentiful supply of meat and dairy produce. Diet was wholesome, if not very interesting. Apart from home-grown vegetables, Styal workers favoured potatoes, bacon, tea, sugar, milk, bread and butter. They purchased offal and the cheaper cuts of meat from Oak Farm.[34]

During the 1820s Samuel Greg also developed various community facilities. For the Quarry Bank operatives, life revolved around the village and the mill. A school, chapels and a shop were all added and

Norcliffe Chapel

societies flourished. These included a Female Society – no doubt Hannah Greg's idea, and a debating society.[35] Audubon, the American artist and naturalist, was a guest of the Gregs in 1826. He was most impressed by the quality of debate that he heard in the village and recalled in his journal:

... I accompanied the two brothers [Samuel Jr and William] to a debating club instituted on their premises for their workmen; on the way we passed a chapel and a low row of cottages for the workpeople and finally reached the schoolroom, where about 30 men had assembled. The question present was 'which was the more advantageous, the discovery of the compass or that of the art of printing.' I listened with interest and later talked with the men on some of the wonders of my own country in which they seemed much interested ... [36]

Samuel Greg's efforts were reinforced by his son. Robert Hyde Greg encouraged the existing societies, sometimes expanding them, and founded new ones of his own. As a founder of the Mechanics' Institute movement in the 1820s, Greg promoted one in Styal, so that adult

Styal school

Backyards of Oak Cottages

Table 6.2 *Wage rates at Quarry Bank and those in Manchester, 1833–50 (weekly)*

	Class of worker	Average wage				Quarry Bank			
		s	d	s	d	s	d	s	d
1833	Children under 13	3	9	– 4	2	1	0	– 3	0
1833–50	Reelers and winders	8	0	– 9	6	4	0	– 7	0
1834–50	Carding men	13	6	– 16	0	8	0	– 17	0
1834–50	Carding women	8	0			6	6	– 7	0
1838–50	Mule spinning men	16	0	– 22	0	10	0	– 13	0
1838–50	Throstles, women	7	6	– 10	6	6	0	– 7	0
1846–50	Power looms, men ⎱ Power looms, women ⎰	10	0	– 11	0	6	6	– 8	0

Sources: A. L. Bowley, *Wages in the United Kingdom in the nineteenth century* (Cambridge 1900), Table facing p. 119; N. J. Smelser, *Social change and the Industrial Revolution* (London 1959), p. 213; A. Ure, *The cotton manufacture of Great Britain*, Vol. II (Manchester 1836), p. 392; MCL C5/1/15/2–5, wages books; MCL C5/1/16/1–2, age certificate books.

education was extended. The Unitarian and Methodist chapels became the focal points of the community. The Sunday schools flourished. In addition, there were lectures, readings, musical evenings and magic lantern displays at the Unitarian chapel. The annual Congregational party was always popular. The gathering in 1868 was fairly typical, when '. . . at various intervals in the course of the evening the choir sang glees . . . were warmly applauded. Mr Payne read a selection from Charles Dickens and Mr Schofield from Washington Irving.'[37]

Styal was a tranquil village in the mid-nineteenth century, a self-contained community supported by a thriving cotton mill. There were no beerhouses for much of the century, so drunkenness was not a problem.[38] One observer commented that:

. . . a social and industrial life was held together not only by interest but also by duty, by respect and by affection, a life in which masters were not only heads and servants were not only hands, but where there were hearts and minds on both sides alike . . . old and young co-operated, the daughters keeping up a close intercourse with the girls and the sons bringing home the result of their studies and their travels to the boys and men – teaching, lecturing and stimulating.[39]

Whilst hardly an impartial account, this does convey the impression Styal made upon many commentators.

Diverting entertainments and good-quality housing are but part of a successful paternalist's management policy. Whilst keeping the success of Quarry Bank constantly in mind, the Gregs appreciated the issues closest to their workers' hearts. Wages were never very high at Quarry Bank; indeed as Table 6.2 shows, they were generally lower than in Manchester during the 1830s. They remained relatively low throughout the century. Cottage rents at 1s 0d to 2s 6d per week from 1835 to 1850 were, however, also low.[40] Moreover, operatives could grow much of their own food; the price of anything they bought was comparatively low and the quality was good. Thus real living standards in Styal were high. Even more important than the maintenance of a good standard of living was job security. At Styal there was no danger of jobs being lost during depressions. If the mill was working short-time, operatives were not charged full rent (normally stopped out of wages) on their cottages. During the American Civil War, for example, Quarry Bank – like so many mills – was forced to shut down. Thomas Tonge, an ex-Greg employee recalled:

While the mill was shut down they [Robert Hyde Greg and his sons] found the men cotton operatives outwork as labourers on the estate. The youths under 21 usually employed in the factory were sent to the local school, *gratis* to supplement what previous education they had had. The women operatives were rounded up in a sewing school, superintended by my aunt, where materials for women's garments furnished at wholesale cost price were made up by women for themselves. The Greg family did nobly in furnishing employment for all their factory employees. In fact, anything to tide them over hard times without humiliating their pride . . . [41]

When Engels claimed the Gregs at Styal used the cottage system to 'make slaves of the operatives', he ignored this aspect of the 'model' factory.[42] It is true that the Gregs, like most nineteenth-century employers, disliked unions, and actually discouraged them. By providing long-term job security, however, they were giving valuable compensation. This, more than anything, helped to guarantee that their aims of low labour turnover and industrial harmony were achieved.

The Gregs combined paternalism at Styal with other types of management. For example, wages at Quarry Bank were paid at piece rates (as revealed in the wages books) which helped to guarantee productivity. Similarly, bonuses and fines were used to ensure quality or to penalise the careless or those who arrived late for work.

The impact of paternalism on efficiency at Quarry Bank is hard to quantify. That labour turnover was low until the last quarter of the nineteenth century and labour unrest negligible suggests a high degree of success. Labour relations were uniformly good at Quarry

Jane Venables, née Jackson, mill worker

Bank, and the mill was only stopped once by industrial action throughout the whole of the nineteenth century. This was during the Plug Riots of 1842. In August, a crowd of 500 Stockport Chartists marched on Styal and brought the mill to a halt.[43] Although they dispersed without damaging the works, the village shop was looted and Quarry Bank remained idle for a fortnight until the troubles had died down. In the mill towns like Preston and Blackburn bouts of labour unrest recurred during the 1850s and 1860s.[44] These left Quarry Bank untouched. That paternalism contributed to this industrial peace seems indisputable, though isolation from the centres of unrest was a further important contributory factor.

It was not until quite late in the nineteenth century that labour turnover began to rise. The last quarter of the century was dominated by uncertainty at Quarry Bank, and job security could no longer be guaranteed.[45] As fewer and fewer operatives were required, income was eroded and families began to leave Styal. The village began to shrink, and Edward Hyde Greg was more worried about the survival of the enterprise and his outside interests than the factory colony. Thus, many of the societies nurtured by his father and grandfather disappeared. Seeing a deterioration in the village, Henry Philips Greg began to intervene. He was not directly involved with Quarry Bank, but owned a large part of Styal and was an industrial paternalist himself. He now attempted to revitalise the village for the remaining inhabitants. His main contribution was the Village Club. Believing that drunkenness was ' . . . the greatest social curse in this country in as much as to it may be traced nearly all the ills from which the body politic suffers . . . ',[46] he was embarrassed, in 1894, when he inherited the Ship Inn from his father. However, although under an obligation to provide travellers with accommodation, he was not required to sell alcohol. As a result, he devised an ingenious scheme which satisfied his principles and financed a village club in Styal. Rather than ban the sale of beer, he limited all customers to two glasses each. The profits from these sales went to the club – the licensee receiving his income from accommodation and light refreshments. It was built behind the Ship Inn and opened in 1900. There villagers could read, play games, attend lectures, debates and classes and give concerts.[47] The character of Styal and the position of the mill had, however, begun to change. Thus, although the club provided much-needed entertainment in the village, its impact on mill efficiency was very marginal. Nevertheless, it illustrates the Gregs' desire to maintain a paternalistic role in the village and their firm belief in the value of such a relationship.

Henry Philips Greg did not confine himself to Styal; his principal business interests were in Reddish. There he exercised his paternalist ideas with great effect. When he began his career at Albert Mill in 1887, Reddish was little more than a village, which he transformed into a thriving community. As in Styal, he set up a club – The Albert, but because of his involvement in the mill his schemes went much further. Playing fields were added and a recreation room built and, in 1915, he appointed a Welfare Secretary at the mill. A thrift scheme was started, to encourage saving and, after World War I, he opened a dental clinic. A combination of high profitability and good labour relations at Albert Mill suggest that these policies were successful.[48]

The Gregs' labour management policies were highly successful at both Styal and Reddish. By realistically assessing their operatives' interests, they were able to realise the full benefits of paternalism.

Providing housing, of course, placed them in a strong position, but it was their recognition that their workers cared most about job security and the maintenance of reasonable living standards which was the secret of their success. Both sides, as a result, genuinely gained from the bargain. The tragedy of Samuel Greg Jr's experiments at Bollington is that he forgot, or perhaps never fully appreciated, the secret of successful paternalism. His was more of a social experiment than an exercise in business management.

IV Bollington: a social experiment

For many years before going to Bollington, Samuel Greg Jr had been worried by the plight of the labouring classes. Both he and his younger brother, William, believed that it was the appalling conditions in manufacturing towns that led the working classes into vice and drunkenness. The contrast between their lot and those of their contempories at Styal seemed stark. Thus, when he took over Lower-house Mill at Bollington in 1832, Samuel Jr saw it as a chance to experiment. He wished to 'elevate the condition of the labouring classes' so that the operatives would lose ' . . . by degree that restless and migratory spirit which is one of the peculiar characteristics of the manufacturing population'.[49] When he moved to Bollington he found little except ' . . . about 50 cottages, most of them well built and of pretty good size; but in extremely bad repair and wanting many little accommodations, such as water, coalsheds, cupboards etc, which are so essential to cleanliness and comfort . . . '[50] After he had restored the mill – a mere shell when he arrived – he set about recruiting a workforce. Some of these came from Quarry Bank, thus ensuring that he had a nucleus of experienced workers. He believed that by providing his operatives with 'fair wages, comfortable houses, gardens for their vegetables and flowers, schools and other means of improvement for their children, sundry little accommodations in the mill, attention to them when sick or in distress [he] would not raise any individuals among them above their condition . . . but elevate the condition itself . . . '[51] The cottages were modernised and gardens laid out and, in 1834, the Sunday School opened. A sports field was made available and within a year he had equipped it with ' . . . a swing and introduced a game called Les Graces with bowls, a leaping bar, a tight rope and afterwards a seesaw . . . '[52] Samuel hoped that if boys and girls were encouraged to play together, they would develop good manners.

This was, however, just the beginning. He decided that there should also be amusements in the winter, when the sports field could not be used. In the autumn of 1834, drawing and singing classes started: 'The drawing class meets every Saturday evening during the winter from 6 to 7.30 and generally spend half the time drawing and the rest with geography and natural history . . . '[53] Unlike his father and his brother Robert, at Styal, both of whom maintained a distance from their employees, Samuel enthusiastically taught this class of 25 boys and young men himself.

Samuel believed that social harmony, both within and between classes, could be best promoted if employers offered guidance on behaviour as well as housing and recreational facilities. He began holding tea parties for the operatives, inviting those 'whose manners and character mark them as in some degree superior to their fellows, or those who I think with a little notice and encouragement and the advantage of good society may become civilised and polished'.[54] He also established what he referred to as the Order of the Silver Cross:

> . . . to which all girls above the age of 17 or 18 are eligible; this ornament became a distinct mark of superiority of character and manner, which it is an object of great ambition to obtain and which has been a most powerful weapon in my hand to forward my great object in refining the minds and manners of our cottage maidens and through their influence of softening and humanizing the sterner part of our population.[55]

One ex-employee at Lowerhouse Mill recalled these early days at Bollington 'Eh! Those were happy days. We used to want the morning to come that we might get back to our work; we felt more as if we were going to school or something like that, we were all so happy and comfortable together . . . '[56] Samuel Jr may have achieved some of his aims, but his idealism had blinded him to the true interests of his employees. Any threat to their job security could lead them to forget about his efforts on their behalf. In 1846, he introduced some new stretching machinery which his workers saw as a threat. They came out on strike, which was a shattering blow. He felt that he had been betrayed and that his schemes were worthless and, in 1847, he suffered a nervous breakdown as a result and abandoned the mill for good.

With hindsight, it is clear that Samuel Jr's plans were both idealistic and over-ambitious. Whilst almost certainly influenced by Robert Owen, he missed one of Owen's key messages. Not only did he forget the importance of job security, but he also overlooked the fundamental relationship between paternalism and profitability. His schemes were useless without a profitable mill. Even without the 1846 strike Samuel's plans were doomed, because his obsession with his social experiment led him to neglect the mill. Profitability declined during the 1840s and he ran into debt, and only the intervention of his brothers saved him from bankruptcy. Ironically, by concentrating so hard on his employees' welfare he was ultimately doing them a disservice; he was threatening not only his own schemes but also their livelihood.

As an integral part of business policy, paternalism could be a useful management tool. An employer trying to improve labour efficiency faced several options. He could threaten fines and dismissal. Alternatively, he could try to influence his employees more subtly. An arrangement emphasising the mutual self-interest of employers and employed could be beneficial. The Gregs at Styal and Reddish were enthusiastic and fully appreciated the potential of the policy. At Bollington, however, Samuel Greg Jr's efforts failed because of his commitment to a social, rather than a business experiment.

CHAPTER 7

Politics

The erosion of traditional political and economic values began in the eighteenth century and continued throughout the nineteenth. Many factors, economic, social and ideological account for the decline of the old society, but easily the most important was the industrial revolution. Its immediate impact upon the distribution of wealth was small, as were the changes in the organisation of the industry as a whole. Yet, ultimately, the developments of the late eighteenth and early nineteenth centuries led to the fundamental shift in the nature of industry, the economy and society as a whole. As the commercial and industrial groups grew in wealth, so did their interest in political issues, especially those which affected them directly. Nevertheless until 1870, for a variety of reasons, relatively few industrialists entered Parliament.[1] Most businessmen were more interested in local problems than wider issues, and only became involved nationally when they were personally affected. Moreover, although the 1832 Reform Act enfranchised the middle classes and guaranteed the representation of the new industrial areas, it did not provide for the payment of Members of Parliament. During this period, few industrialists were wealthy enough to allow themselves the luxury of entering Parliament. As a result, the entrepreneurs who did were generally from long-established commercial and industrial families like the Philipses and the Gregs. Additionally, as with Robert Hyde Greg, who was Manchester's Anti-Corn Law Member of Parliament from 1839–42, businessmen were often Members of Parliament for short periods, during specific agitations.

For much of the nineteenth century, the Gregs, like many Nonconformist buisnessmen, were Liberals though never Radicals. Their views on such issues as reform of the franchise, repeal of the Corn Laws and Factory Reform reflected the interests of the commercial and manufacturing community of which they were part. Even William

123

Rathbone Greg, who abandoned business whilst still quite a young man, never lost his allegiance to the commercial groups.

Samuel Sr's interest in politics was strictly peripheral and largely passive. As a prominent member of the Manchester business community, with a keen interest in the success of his firm, his name is regularly to be found among petitioners who pressurised the government on trading policies. An unreformed Parliament, combined with a natural reserve and a single-minded devotion to his firm, limited his activities to petitions and attending meetings. His sons, especially Robert and William, were far less inhibited. Robert was an energetic member of the Manchester Chamber of Commerce, the Reform Movement and the Anti-Corn Law League. His political activity was, however, short-lived and was really an extension of his business interests. William, on the other hand, although never a successful parliamentary candidate, became a prolific political writer of some repute.

I Reform of the electoral system

Before and during the industrial revolution, society was based upon the principles of property, patronage and privilege. The ownership of property and, more especially, land, in pre-industrial England determined an individual's position in society, the extent of his duties and the nature of the privileges he enjoyed.[2] One of the inevitable privileges and indeed duties of the landowning classes was government. Prior to 1832 and indeed for many years after, Parliament was dominated by the landed aristocracy. Their ownership of property meant that, traditionally, it was they who made the decisions for the good of the majority. In reality, by the eighteenth century Parliament was not only corrupt and increasingly unrepresentative, but its policies favoured the landed groups. Criticism grew. It was not, however, until the beginning of the nineteenth century that pressure for change increased dramatically. Representation did not reflect the demographic and industrial changes of the late eighteenth century, being biased towards landed property rather than industry or population. As a result the burgeoning industrial towns of Birmingham and Manchester were without a voice in Parliament, while the traditionally prosperous agricultural counties of the south were over-represented.[3]

Demands for reform varied. The goal of many radicals was full manhood suffrage, whilst others were in favour of more limited reforms which would create representation for the industrial areas, though retaining property qualifications for voters. The ending of the

Napoleonic Wars and the passage of the notorious Corn Laws led to concerted action. Middle and working classes were, for a short while, united in their attacks on the landed Parliament, which strove to keep grain prices high and so protect its own interests. Pressure continued throughout the 1820s. Reform, when it came, must have been a sad disappointment to the working-class groups. There was nothing radical about the 1832 Reform Act, and any short-lived illusion of unity between the middle and working classes was lost. The Act removed the anomaly of under-representation in the new centres of wealth by redistributing seats, but it retained the age-old respect for property. The vote was granted to the £10 householder, the £10 copyholder and the long leaseholder in towns, as well as the £50 short leaseholders and tenants-at-will in towns. In this way only relatively few were added to the electorate – the newly propertied, the industrial and commercial middle classes. It was within these groups that strongest opposition to the 1867 Reform Act arose, for it reduced the property qualification.

The Greg family, like many of their contemporaries in Manchester in the 1820s, were energetic supporters of electoral reform. Robert Hyde Greg, at this time an eager young man prepared to spend long hours not just working in his father's firm but also attending political meetings, was adamant that what he termed 'the present monstrous system of elective franchise'; should be changed. At a reform meeting in Manchester, in 1831, he argued convincingly '. . . that members must no longer be allowed to elect themselves – that principle must be introduced where there is none – and in short that the elective franchise should be so efficient that members of the House of Commons should be really not nominally the representatives of the people'.[4] With this objective achieved, both Robert and his younger brother, William, remained staunch supporters of the secret ballot and the further removal of rotten boroughs.[5] There, however, their enthusiasm for further reform ended. William, especially, was a confirmed anti-democrat. Amongst the middle though not the working classes, thoughts of further reform were lost amidst the excitement generated for over a decade by the Anti-Corn Law campaign. In 1846, with victory secured, it was Cobden who, aware of the success of the Anti-Corn Law subscription fund, tried to revive it (and the support of the manufacturers) for the reform of the franchise. A radical, he misjudged his former supporters, as William Rathbone Greg wrote to him in 1848:

. . . I am fearful lest you, not knowing the extent to which . . . laziness, modesty and unwillingness to state their dissent from the opinions of a man so much respected and a party with whom they have so long acted . . . should be led to believe that the concurrence of the old reformers in the movement is much more general than it really is . . . I have had much conversation of late with many who went heart and hand with you in the League struggle . . . and I have found them unanimous in condemning the peculiar time and object chosen for the new agitation. Not only do they feel that the attempt to revive the organization of the League for other purposes is a mistake which cannot but discredit the judgement and singlemindedness of motive of the former agit...ion but they think the time unwise and the cause questionable.[6]

That he was echoing the views of the majority of manufacturers is clear from the few that ultimately supported Cobden. Robert Hyde Greg was likewise opposed to further change. In stark contrast to his views on the benefits of the 1832 reform, any further extension of suffrage would, he believed, devalue property and lead to corruption and extremism. He wrote in his journal in the late 1840s:

. . . the lower we descend [in conferring the franchise] the more necessary ignorance for the majority, [since much time] must be spent in providing for existence, not acquiring knowledge. The poverty causes dependence and is easily bought. No property diminishes respect for property, consequently the security of property becomes compromised. Multitudes are easily carried away by passion and . . . by rumours however absurd.[7]

There were several abortive attempts at further reform, which elicited uniformly hostile responses from William Rathbone Greg. In two letters to Gladstone, in 1852, he proclaimed himself a confirmed anti-democrat and alarmed by the enfranchisement of uneducated classes. Thus, in April 1852 he wrote:

I am one of a considerable and daily increasing class who belong to a liberal party by early connection, long and active association and by many surviving opinions also, who are yet decidedly conservative on all that relates to the further infusion of the democratic element into our constitution. We still consider ourselves earnest reformers, but thorough anti-democrats![8]

While four months later he expressed the belief that Russell's Reform Bill of 1852 would lead '. . . ineluctably though perhaps gradually to universal or at least household suffrage: that such conclusion as it would transfer the power from the educated classes to the comparatively uneducated, not merely admit the latter to a share – is now and always inadmissible . . .'[9] By 1867 William felt little remaining sympathy with the Liberal party and was horrified at the new Reform Act. A firm believer in the doctrine of self-help, he was convinced that the new legislation removed the incentive to acquire property and undermined the very fabric of society. He wrote 'The Reform Bill of 1867 takes the command of representation out of the hands of the

William Rathbone Greg

propertied classes and puts it in the hands of the wage receiving classes. It gives it over from the upper and middle ranks of the community to lower ranks. It transfers electoral preponderance from property to proletariat from capital to labour.'[10] How similar were his fears and prejudices to those of the aristocracy, forty years earlier! To both Robert and William the solution lay not in the removal of the property qualification, but in the universal provision of education. Recent research has shown that their attitude was widely shared among cotton manufacturers.[11]

William Rathbone Greg's view, whilst extreme, more so certainly than that of his brother, Samuel, and possibly even than that of Robert, reflected the philosophy of one brought up in a wealthy nineteenth-century commercial family. He admitted, as a young man, that factory owners should bear the responsibility for appalling urban conditions.[12] Similarly, his mill had been managed on paternalistic lines, but like many such employers he felt little natural allegiance with working people. As John Morley, Cobden's biographer, said of him 'For the miseries of the working class, Mr Greg's pity was profound and almost passionate, but his moral and intellectual sympathy was not with them and was often inaccessible, from their point of view.'[13] William's biting attack on Mrs Gaskell, a family friend, for what he saw as her misleading descriptions of both millowners and operatives in *Mary Barton*, highlights his antipathy to many of the working class. At the same time, it articulates his faith in self-help:

How came it never to occur to the authoress [he wrote bitterly] or to her hero that had Mr Carson (who is represented as having raised himself from the operative class) thought as little of saving as John Barton who so envied and so wronged him, their condition and suffering when the period of distress arrived would have been precisely equal . . .[14]

II Free trade

The opposition of businessmen to their predominantly aristocratic rulers did not end with reform of the electoral system. An issue even closer to their hearts and one which served to galvanise their agitation for the Reform Act, was free trade. In 1772 Adam Smith argued in *The Wealth of Nations* that the monopolies and restrictions to trade, which were so much part of eighteenth-century commercial policy, far from producing prosperity hampered development. National wealth, he believed, was increased by specialisation based upon comparative advantage. Only if trade was unrestricted could countries produce goods, whether primary products or manufactured goods in which they had a comparative advantage. Such was the ideological basis of support for free trade. This philosophy underlay all Victorian economic and social policy. Manufacturers were readily attracted to the doctrine of free trade, since in it lay the key to wider markets, invaluable at a time when the home market was limited. Moreover, most of them believed that protection benefited the landed groups at their expense. Nevertheless, their support for free trade sometimes wavered if it could damage their interests. Thus, for seventeen years the manufacturing interests opposed the export of machinery, only giving way in the hope of encouraging repeal of the Corn Laws.

Many prominent Manchester businessmen, including the Philipses, the Ashworths, George Wilson, the Gregs and most of the Chamber of Commerce flung themselves wholeheartedly into the Anti-Corn Law agitations. Agriculture had thrived during the Napoleonic War period. Demand for food, not just from the army but from Britain's allies, cut off from their traditional sources of supply, was artificially high, leading to soaring prices and correspondingly inflated rents. In an effort to protect farmers and landowners from inevitably declining prices, following the peace, the Corn Law was passed in 1815. It introduced duties which prohibited the importation of foreign grain until the domestic price had reached a certain level. The landed groups thus sought to protect agriculture artificially by inhibiting foreign competition. At a stroke they alienated middle- and working-class groups alike, whilst political economists were increasingly supporting free trade. The commercial and industrial classes, especially the textile producers, were increasingly aware of the potential benefits of free trade to a nation with a near-monopoly in the production of manufactured goods. By closing British markets to the world's primary producers, they argued, the government was also restricting the markets for the country's manufactured goods and even encouraging foreign competition. Moreover, these groups saw no reason to subsidise the activities of the landed groups and support inefficiency.

To the working class, the effect of the Corn Laws was simple. They artificially inflated bread prices and thus reduced living standards. There was, however, little unity of action between the two groups. Mutual mistrust, not reduced by the First Reform Act, precluded joint efforts. For many of the moderate Anti-Corn Law Leaguers, any working-class action was associated with Chartism. Most Chartists, on the other hand, scorned the League as being dominated by middle-class businessmen who would, once food prices were reduced, have the excuse to reduce wages in line with Ricardian wages theory. The working classes would, therefore, reap no benefit from the change.[15]

Agitation for the repeal of the Corn Laws, muted at first, began almost as soon as the duties were introduced, particularly within the business community. Throughout the 1820s the members of the Manchester Chamber of Commerce repeatedly condemned the laws and championed free trade.[16] The first step towards repeal came in 1828, when a sliding scale of duties replaced absolute prohibition of imported grain. The way this operated was simple: the duty on foreign grain was highest when home prices were low; as they rose, so duty paid on imported corn declined. This measure was followed by some apparent loss of interest in the campaign. Instead, the champions of repeal were more concerned with electoral reform. It was a severe depression which finally stimulated a concerted attack on the Corn

Laws. The Anti-Corn Law League was set up in Manchester in 1838 to campaign for repeal. Numerous cotton manufacturers joined, eager to overcome growing economic ills through the wider markets offered by free trade. Membership of the League was by subscription, many industrialists being happy to contribute capital to a fund which ultimately topped £80,000 in the belief that the returns would be impressive.[17] Indeed, one Liverpool merchant was especially optimistic about the potential rewards from his investment, stating at a meeting in 1842 that:

> He had gladly given his £100 for the next year to accomplish the objects of the League; he had hopes he was promoting his own individual goods to no small extent by extending free trade principles; he was not ashamed to avow his belief that his £100 subscription would bring him back a hundred times £100 if the objects of the League should happen to be attended with success.[18]

The rhetoric of Cobden and Bright swayed thousands, but without the financial support and tireless activity of manufacturers, inspired as they were by self-interest, the campaign was unlikely to succeed. The agitation surpassed even the reform movement in its scale, and whilst other issues, such as the ending of the slave trade, captured the national imagination, no previous campaign had been of comparable scope. In 1846 the League achieved its objective and the era of free trade began.

That neither the hopes of the commercial groups nor the fears of the aristocracy were fully realised is sometimes forgotten. Repeal of the Corn Laws did usher in a period of economic prosperity. The mid-Victorian boom, from 1850 until 1873, whilst neither universal nor uninterrupted, saw some sectors of industry enjoying rising profits. Ironically, the benefits were felt less by the cotton manufacturers, who had campaigned so vigorously for repeal, than by the producers of pig iron and other capital goods, whose exports grew as primary producers developed their railway networks to transport grain in response to widening markets. At the same time food prices did not immediately plummet, as feared by the landed groups. It was not until the conclusion of the American Civil War, in 1865, when the prairies began to be fully exploited, that imported grain began to depress domestic prices in the United Kingdom. Similarly, it was not until this period, when the cost of basic foodstuffs declined, that some working-class groups began to experience rising living standards.

The Greg family's faith in the free market resembled that of their contemporaries. Prominent in Manchester commercial society, with the fortunes of a large and thriving firm to promote, it was inevitable that they played a leading role in an agitation so important to the interests of the textile community. From the late eighteenth century onwards, the Gregs supported to varying degrees the principle of free trade and removal of monopoly. They made little pretence of ideological commitment. They were prepared to work energetically to secure an end which would improve their profit levels, but when free trade interfered with their interests, they could be equally vehement in opposition.

It was during the late eighteenth century, not long after going into business, that Samuel Greg first expressed a dislike of trade restrictions and monopoly. In a letter to William Rathbone he complained bitterly about the East India Company:

Our instructions are to ask for the liberty of trading in those seas as British subjects of exporting and importing and not to accede to the proposition that ye company shall be our carriers. I have really now hoped that this important business will be fairly and generally discussed and the interest of the body kingdom weighed against that of a few rapacious and corrupt individuals.[19]

The campaign for trade liberalisation was, however, in its infancy in the 1790s, and did not gather momentum for thirty years. Samuel was thus content to attend a few meetings and pledge his support to petition when required. He was an old man by the 1830s and left it to his sons to campaign tirelessly for a cause close to his heart.

When members of the Manchester Chamber of Commerce started to argue in favour of free trade during the 1820s, Robert Hyde Greg gave enthusiastic support. In 1825 he drew up a memorial outlining the benefits of free trade and, in the next year, began arguing that the Corn Laws should be repealed.[20] For the next fifteen years he helped to spearhead the campaign which ultimately changed the face of Britain's commercial policy for nearly a century. As he wrote to his son, Robert, in 1843, his interest in the issue pre-dated even that of Cobden: 'The fact is that no one in Lancashire some years ago thought anything about the Corn Laws except J. B. Smith and myself. Cobden was then unknown but the second time I ever saw him was when he came to me, in the company of J. B. Smith for the purpose of forming an Anti-Corn Law Association . . .'[21] When the Association gave way in 1838 to the nationally organised League both Robert and, to a lesser extent, William Rathbone Greg were energetic campaigners. Unlike many manufacturers, whose only contribution was money for the subscription fund, they both devoted a great deal of time to the League. They attended and spoke at numerous meetings, dinners and tea parties to support the cause of the Repeal of the Corn Laws. Concurrently, Robert was exhausting himself trying to co-ordinate and manage the family business – at times, it seems, almost single-handed. He neared a breakdown in 1839 and went abroad to recover. During his absence the League nominated him for a vacant Manchester parliamentary seat without, it seems, consulting him. He was elected to the House of Commons, *in absentia*, without attending a single husting. Although annoyed and not a little dismayed at the prospect of serving at Westminster, Greg took his seat. His loyalty to a cause which he believed would give an invaluable stimulus to manufacturing was such that he felt he had no choice. He remained a Member of Parliament until 1841.

Robert Hyde Greg's support for repeal of the Corn Laws was practical rather than ideological. Well versed in the philosophy of Adam Smith, he used it to attack the agricultural groups who, he believed, were protected to the detriment of the country as a whole and manufacturers in particular. 'Agriculture', he argued at a meeting in 1840, 'has relied upon protection instead of relying as it ought to have done on intelligence, frugality and industry.'[22] Continuing this theme in his journal, he wrote:

What right has the landed interest or rather the landlords to exclusive or unequal protection? Have the 50,000 the consent of the 25 millions to pay them a high price for their food and continue to pay them. What right have the owners of land to say to the owners of every other kind of property 'We demand preference over you.'[23]

Such abhorrence of protection and the inefficiency he believed it created led him, as an improving landlord, to publish pamphlets on agricultural improvement. These not only discussed new techniques but also pointed to the waste in prevailing methods. This, he argued, was the natural consequence of undue protection.[24] His attack on the Corn Laws was many-pronged, for he also pointed in 1843 to the impact which they had on trade:

The great point we have to impress upon the minds of our rulers is that trade is merely barter, that it is simply an exchange of one commodity for another, that we can no more trade with those countries the products of which we refuse to receive than we can trade with those countries which absolutely prohibit the products of this country.[25]

Robert's support for repeal remained unswerving throughout the campaign. Towards the end, however, he faded into the background of the League and attended fewer and fewer meetings. Whether this was simply a consequence of increasing pressures of work, or indifferent health, or a difference in approach from that of men like Cobden, it is hard to tell. He remained a moderate throughout and was increasingly alarmed by the tactics and proposals of the more radical

Leaguers who became prominent in the early 1840s. In 1842 he wrote to George Wilson:

... I consider the present disturbances to be properly styled, a Chartist insurrection and if the Anti-Corn Law League were to join in it would end in Revolution. Surely, at this moment nothing should be thought of by every good subject but restoring peace and order, that done let them bring their accusations against the League. You know as well as myself how carefully we have avoided the remotest breach of the law and how little we have to fear.[26]

For whatever reason, he became less and less active in the Movement and, when Repeal was secured in 1846, he showed no further interest in politics.

His younger brother, William, too young to be in the forefront of the early agitation nevertheless shared Robert's sympathy for repeal. William's approach differed from Robert's to the extent that he has been labelled among the 'humanitarian' supporters of free trade.[27] He argued that high bread prices were causing considerable distress, declaring at a meeting in 1842:

That this meeting has learned with greatest indignation, that the sufferings of the working classes and the embarrassments of their employers in manufac-turing districts will receive no alleviation from any measure to be proposed to parliament by the present parliament, that their distress is met by an insulting proposal to perpetuate the bread tax and thereby keep up the first necessary of life at a famine price.[28]

Later in the same year he elaborated on his views in a Prize Essay on the Corn Laws, followed by a persuasive paper in which he developed a convincing theory of under-consumption. High agricultural prices, he argued, reduced the money which the mass of the population could spend on manufactured goods. This meant that manufacturers faced deficient demand and were forced to reduce production. The inevitable consequence was bankruptcy for some employers and unemployment and hardship among operatives. At a time when Lancashire was suffering from one of the severest depressions of the century, his views were given a fair degree of credence, though not by the government.[29] Like his brother, Robert, William continued to support the League until repeal was achieved but, rather than with-drawing from politics, he became increasingly vocal and produced numerous pamphlets on subjects ranging from Reform to Karl Marx.[30]

Free trade was thus seen by the Gregs as the key to economic prosperity leading to widening markets, lower food prices and greater agricultural efficiency. The free market did not always work in their favour, however, as in the case of the export of yarn in the late eighteenth century and machinery in the 1820s and 1830s. In these instances the Gregs, keen to protect their business, were as enthusiastic in their support of protection as in their cries for general free trade. In 1794 Samuel Greg – then a cloth-producer – attended a meeting of the Society of Merchants in Manchester which declared:

> ... the evils arising from the exportation of cotton yarn are manifold. It is evident that it must enhance the price of this article to our manufacturers and the general tendency of this proved injurious to the sale of our goods. The more foreign manufacturers become acquainted with the superior properties of our yarn, the greater will be their endeavours to obtain our machinery and it is well known how easily foreigners succeed in pursuits of this kind.[31]

The family were, however, even more disturbed by the implications of the free export of machinery, when it was suggested in 1825. They foresaw heightened foreign competition and the erosion of Britain's strong position in international markets. Many other manufacturers felt similarly and, in 1826, Robert Hyde Greg moved at a special General Meeting of the Manchester Chamber of Commerce:

> We admit to the full extent the principles of Free Trade – we would support no exclusive monopolies of raw produce and manufacturers – we would sustain no unprofitable trade by bounties or prohibitory duties – we would draw our supplies from the cheapest sources – but nevertheless we would not export the machinery employed in our staple manufactures to enable other nations to undersell us in foreign markets.[32]

Greg reluctantly supported the removal of export restrictions on machinery in 1842 but maintained his position on the consequences of the move. In 1846 he declared to a Parliamentary Select Committee:

> ... the competition is much keener. Machinery abroad is about thirty per cent higher in price and in some places about fifty per cent worse in quality and though patterns have been occasionally exported, and there have been a few machines smuggled that it is a very different thing from having machinery ready made on the best principles from the machine shop here ...'[33]

Far from being a contradiction of his beliefs, this illustrates how closely Greg's political interests were allied to his business. They were one and the same thing.

III Factory reform

An issue even closer to the hearts of cotton manufacturers than either electoral reform or repeal of the Corn Laws, was state interference in factory hours and control of conditions in mills. Unfettered by legislative controls in the eighteenth century many, though by no means all, millowners abused their position. Operatives, many of whom were children from parish poorhouses, sometimes worked excessively long hours in appalling conditions. By the end of the eighteenth century public disquiet was sufficient to encourage legislation. It was Sir Robert Peel, one of the largest employers of poor children, who introduced what was effectively the first Factory Act, in 1802.[34] This legislation, which limited the hours worked by parish apprentices in cotton mills to 12 daily, was in 1819 extended to all children working in cotton mills.[35] Further adjustments were made in both 1825 and 1831. It was, however, during the 1830s and 1840s that the most dramatic moves towards factory reform and the restriction of hours were made. In 1833 the Factory Act, which applied to most textile mills, reduced the working day for those under sixteen years of age to 69 hours a week (a maximum of 12 hours in any day with 9 on Saturdays). For children between the ages of ten to thirteen there was to be an 8-hour day, and such children were to be educated at schools provided by their employers. Factory inspectors were appointed to monitor mill-owners' compliance with the Act.[36]

Public interest in factories had been re-awakened by the Factory Inquiry Commission, which preceded the 1833 Act. As a result, commentators concentrated much of their attention on mill conditions and urban squalor. Writers like Peter Gaskell and Friedrich Engels wrote about the evils of the factory system and the ills which were attributable to it whilst a few, such as Andrew Ure, made valiant attempts to defend it.[37] The Ten Hours movement, born in the 1820s, gathered momentum and found support in some strange quarters. The landed classes used factory conditions to attack the manufacturers during the Corn Law agitation. The manufacturers saw legislation as unwelcome government interference which would serve to reduce their profit margins and place them in an unfavourable position in respect of foreign rivals.[38] They viewed the Ten Hours Movement with the utmost suspicion, seeing it as part of an attack on their position by elements in the working classes. Despite their opposition the Ten Hours Movement achieved its objective in 1847 and total working hours were reduced to 58. This applied not just to children and young people, as before, but to women as well.[39] The reduction of the working day in textile factories was a recognition by the government of a need to yield to some working-class demands in a decade of exceptional turmoil, both at home and abroad. By 1850, the fire had gone out of the unrest and two hours were added to the working day without a murmur from the operatives' leaders.

Robert Hyde Greg was incensed by the government's interference in factory hours and held the Ten Hours Movement in contempt. He was in favour of the 1802 and 1819 legislation and was prepared to recognise some merit in the 1833 Act. Any further reduction of hours would, he believed, be damaging to all concerned, since output would be cut. Angered by an article which appeared in the Tory *Quarterly Review* in 1836, he was roused to write a defence of the factory system. In *The factory question*, which appeared in 1837, his dislike of legislation and the Ten Hours Movement is clear.[40] As a manufacturer whose family had long provided far more than the minimum conditions laid down by any of the Factory Acts, he resented any outside interference. Had he, however, shown less prejudice against the Ten Hours Movement and more readiness to accept that some millowners abused their positions and that urban conditions were atrocious, he might have received a more sympathetic hearing. As it was, by deriding the Ten Hours Movement and even denouncing his brother William's paper on urban conditions as a 'mere college thesis' not worthy of credence, he invited the scorn of his opponents.[41] Response came the following year in an anonymous pamphlet, probably written by John Doherty. In it Greg was mocked for hypocrisy and inaccuracy.[42] By then, however, Greg was too ill to respond, though the exchange had naturally reinforced his antipathy towards the Ten Hours Movement. For the rest of his life he was distrustful of organised labour and suspicious of factory legislation. Many years later in 1855, as chairman of the *National Association of Factory Occupiers*, he spearheaded opposition amongst millowners to the fencing of horizontal shafting. He saw it as yet another example of the interference of the pseudo-philanthropists.[43]

William Rathbone Greg also disliked factory legislation and deplored trade unions. He believed, for example, that the Preston strike of 1853–4 was the result of the successful campaign to reduce the working day. Thus, in a letter to the *Economist*, he wrote:

No one acquainted with the factory districts can doubt that the present strikes are mainly attributable to the agitation for the present factory act. In every principal town, the centre of factory districts, a paid committee existed fostered and flattered by some important personages in parliament. These men, after obtaining the alterations in the law required by them and their supporters, turned their attention to other subjects likely to engage the attention of the masses . . .[44]

His suspicion and dislike of trade unions increased as he got older and many of his later publications concentrated on this theme.[45]

The Gregs wasted little time and effort on mere ideology. In politics, as in business, they were realists and each issue was assessed on its merits. Their principal concern remained the welfare of their business and the position of the manufacturing class in society. Believing that nineteenth-century prosperity was the result of their (and other industrialists') efforts, they fought hard to guarantee the rewards they believed were due to them and to protect their interests. Their politics in the nineteenth century and those of the manufacturers were unashamedly the politics of self-interest, at the time the most effective weapon against the self-interest of an aristocratic Parliament. That they were apparently blind to the interests of the working classes was the result, in part at least, of their commitment to paternalism. They were not merely cynical profit maximisers, but genuinely believed that they understood the operatives' needs best. Moreover, as caring employers and property owners, they were in a position to help them towards better education without which, the Gregs believed, workers could not and should not make decisions for themselves. Until the working classes were adequately educated, they felt it was inconceivable that they could make impartial decisions for themselves.

EPILOGUE

For four generations the Gregs were involved with Quarry Bank and guided life in Styal. Samuel Greg's sons and grandsons had, all in their different ways, ensured a degree of continuity, though enforced entry into the family firm had created difficulties. By the 1930s, a world war and changing economic conditions meant that the family's links with Styal and the industry in which they had made their fortune began to be severed.

On the eve of World War I Quarry Bank was struggling to regain solvency, whilst at the Albert Mill expansion was continuing apace. Ernest William, Henry Philips and Robert Alexander all made Styal their home, their influence over the village resembling that of their forebears. The First World War, however, shattered a generation and turned life upside down, even in a small village like Styal.

Styal War Memorial starkly records the impact of the war on the community. Thirteen men died, including two of Ernest William Greg's sons, who were killed within thirteen months of each other. Arthur Greg had just completed his first year at Oxford when war broke out. He volunteered immediately and held a commission with the Sherwood Foresters. His vivid letters written shortly before he was wounded at the second Battle of Ypres capture the horrors of the front line. During 1915 he wrote:

After a good many halts we finally came to the end of that shell-swept two miles of open country. It was piping hot and we were terribly thirsty. The sights we saw on the way up were not calculated to cheer us much. We passed many groups of men, dead or dying some wounded and all badly gassed. Most of them were writhing in awful agony . . . [1]

Not long after, he was wounded himself. His description, whilst chilling, demonstrated a wry sense of humour:

I went down like a log and was aware of a loose, horrid and disconnected feeling about the lower half of my face. I was bleeding like a fountain and my

Departure for World War I: Thomas Venables (a Quarry Bank employee) fourth from right

mouth seemed full of obstacles. I tried to spit them out and found they were teeth. I remember distinctly some fellow saying in an agonised whisper, 'He's had his false teeth knocked out.' This annoyed me horribly as I had always been proud of my teeth . . . [2]

Arthur recovered and, in 1917, joined the Royal Flying Corps and was killed returning from a bombing raid. His sister, Madge, was the last member of the family to see him alive. A VAD nurse from 1915, Madge had been stationed in various parts of Northern France. She kept a diary and on 17 April 1917, recorded ' . . . wet morning was alone on duty at 4 p.m. when . . . Arthur walked in'.[3] They dined together. Twelve days later she received a wire from home telling her that he had been killed. In May 1918, just six months before the Armistice, her second brother, Robert, was also killed.

The late nineteenth and early twentieth centuries were characterised, for the Greg family, by a contraction in their cotton interests. Increasingly, the family pursued alternative careers. Of Edward Hyde Greg's six sons (see Figure E.1) only two – Ernest William and Robert

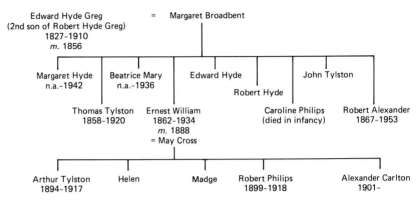

Figure E.1   The later Gregs: descendants of Edward Hyde Greg

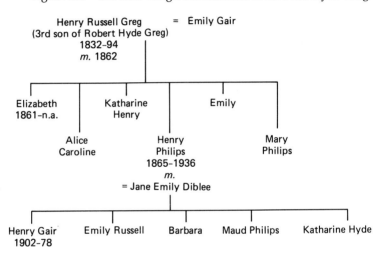

Figure E.2   The later Gregs: descendants of Henry Russell Greg

Alexander – were involved in the cotton industry, whilst their cousin, Henry Philips Greg (see Figure E.2), Henry Russell's only son, continued at Reddish. Ernest William had followed his uncle, Arthur, into Chadwicks, while Robert Alexander continued to guide Quarry Bank until the 1920s. Alexander, Ernest's only surviving son, had no desire to go into the cotton industry, and he could not have earned an adequate living from Quarry Bank, had he wished to. Instead, in 1926, he left Styal to farm near Northwich in Cheshire. His father and uncle turned Quarry Bank into a limited company in 1923,[4] and whilst remaining principal shareholders, withdrew into the background. They consigned the mill's management to Samuel Henshall, a pre-war employee. Henshall remained there until the mill closed, more than thirty years later.

That Quarry Bank continued to operate for so long is a tribute to Samuel Henshall's ingenuity and the Gregs' perception of the mill almost as a charitable institution. There was little economic justification for its continued operation, beyond 1900. Yet, at that time, its closure would have been devastating for the tiny community at Styal, which still relied heavily on the mill for employment. That it was able to continue in the 1920s and 1930s owes much to Samuel Henshall's skill as a manager. Trained after the First World War as a cost accountant, he guided the mill through the difficult inter-war years.

A combination of factors reduced the size of Britain's overseas markets for cotton goods and eroded competitiveness. Import substitution during World War I (especially in India and Japan), reduced the size of Far Eastern markets for cotton goods. Declining primary product prices, on the other hand, reduced the incomes of many of Britain's major customers.[5] This was not all, however: the British cotton industry was ceasing to be competitive. Some have argued that this was the result of resistance to new technology.[6] The debate is, however, inconclusive, since it may be that the decline of the cotton industry in the later stages of economic development is inevitable. For a few efficient modernised mills, the period was challenging. For an archaic concern, like Quarry Bank, it was an upward struggle.

By the 1930s, there were still 178 operatives employed at Quarry Bank.[7] By then, however, calico weaving – the mill's mainstay for almost a hundred years, was no longer viable because of foreign competition. Anxious to avoid closure, Henshall examined the alternatives. He faced significant financial constraints and solved the problem by modifying the looms so that laundry bags could be produced. Just before the outbreak of the Second World War, after much painstaking work, production began. The war and resultant conscription into the armed forces meant that the labour force shrank and never recovered. In 1950 only 13 operatives remained and nine years later Quarry Bank closed.

Long before production ceased at Quarry Bank, the family's relationship with Styal changed. Ernest William and Henry Philips Greg died in 1934 and 1936 respectively. Ernest had lived at Norcliffe Hall from 1910, commuting daily to Bolton. His cousin had lived on the other side of the Styal Estate at Lode Hill, the house built for his father in the 1860s. Both retained a paternalistic interest in the village. Ernest's death was the end of an era for Styal and for the family. As Robert Alexander commented to his nephew, 'The death of your father represents to me the end of the old life for the Greg family. Your father was the only one who had the inclination and financial and natural ability to carry out the duties and responsibilities of a head of the family . . . '[8] Not wishing to return to Styal himself and having no involvement with Quarry Bank, Ernest's son, Alexander, was faced with the disposal of the estate. A plan by Wilmslow Council to build houses on part of it persuaded him to offer a portion of the land (including Quarry Bank Mill, the village and surrounding woodland) to the National Trust. The transaction was completed in 1939.

To an organisation used to the administration of country estates, and industrial site, however rural, proved an anomaly. For many years the property's future remained uncertain. For a while, after weaving ceased, the mill was sub-let to small businesses. In the late 1960s, however, the need to repair the mill became pressing, for the ivy-clad building was crumbling and the timbers were riddled with rot. Over £150,000 was spent on renovation though, even then, the mill's future remained uncertain. Interest in Britain's industrial heritage was, however, growing and the idea of a textile museum was born. Quarry Bank, a water-powered mill founded at the dawn of the industrial revolution, with its adjacent factory village and scenic position, was ideal. In 1975 an independent charitable trust was set up to raise funds for the projected museum and to administer it. After years of idleness, Quarry Bank gradually reawakened and, in June 1978, the first limited exhibition opened. Six years later, as the result of incessant work by a dedicated staff and numerous volunteers, Quarry Bank won the Museum of the Year Award – exactly 200 years after opening as a cotton mill. Quarry Bank's long history mirrors the rise and decline of the British cotton industry. Now, in the era of de-industrialisation, events have come full circle. The mill, which provided wealth for the Gregs and employment for the Styal villagers, now generates interest and entertainment for thousands of visitors each year.

Conclusions

Business historians have been criticised for concentrating too much on the specific and thus deriving few conclusions of relevance to the wider study of economic growth. In this book, it was not intended to draw broad, general conclusions on the basis of a single – far from typical – firm. Instead, by focusing on the development of the Gregs' business interests, the intention has been to show *how* and *why* its experience was different from that of competitors. In this way, it is possible to gain a deeper understanding of the process of industrial change.

Central to any recent history of the cotton industry during the industrial revolution has been the predominance of small firms. Samuel Greg and Company was, by contrast, very large until 1841. A study of how and why it grew adds to the understanding of more normal firms and helps explain why, for most firms, such scale was impractical or even unattainable. Samuel Greg, like many entrepreneurs, wished to provide for his large family. This encouraged him to expand his business. His expansion path was eased and, at times, his very survival ensured by long establishment. This gave him a reputation for high quality, a range of contacts, access to credit (both long and short) and wealth. High bankruptcy rates meant that relatively few firms survived to enjoy such advantages. Those which did – such as the Peels' or the Strutts', for example – grew. It is thus possible that one explanation of the plethora of small firms was that a high proportion of them were relatively new.

Analysis of the timing of the growth of Samuel Greg and Company has revealed some interesting tendencies in the nature of yarn and cloth markets. Discussion of market power in the cotton trade, outside very fine yarns and cloths, has been sadly lacking. The possibility that the products of individual mills, especially at the coarser end of the market, were sufficiently differentiated for manufacturers to derive advantages, has rarely been considered. Yet Quarry Bank yarns dominated highly specialised markets in the post-Napoleonic Wars period, providing the necessary incentive for expansion of production. Similarly, thread spun at the Albert Mill was of sufficiently high quality to be popular on the London market. Additional research is necessary before any sound conclusions can emerge concerning the nature of these markets. Nevertheless, the suspicion remains that a high degree of product differentiation on all types of yarn and cloth must, for much of the nineteenth century, have led to the exertion of substantial market power by leaders of the industry.

Water power, far more than steam, was of great importance to the early development of a factory-based cotton industry. The majority of mills prior to the 1820s were water-powered and rurally based. The running costs of a water-powered system were minimal. Several factors, however, led to a growth in the use of steam engines and to the ultimate demise of the water mill. In the first place, as the scope and complexity of technology increased so, too, did the fixed costs associated with water power. Secondly, the irregularity of supply on many water sites interrupted production. Related to this problem was the growing shortage of good water sites as mills proliferated. Increasingly, therefore, from the 1830s as the efficiency of steam power increased, new mills were run by steam engines. Additionally, as the century progressed many small, marginal mills, especially those on the geographic periphery of the industry, were abandoned. Thus by 1900 only a tiny percentage of the industry's motive power came from water.

The question inevitably arises of why water power continued to be used at Quarry Bank. Throughout, Quarry Bank was an exceptional water site – its capacity undreamed of by Samuel Greg in the 1780s. It lacked the constraints of many rural mills, whilst the absence of other cotton mills on the River Bollin meant that the river's resources were never overtaxed. This helps to explain the phenomenal expansion of water power at the mill during the 1820s. The continued use of the river during the rest of the nineteenth century is not hard to explain. Having incurred heavy fixed expenditure on a water-powered system, it would have been irrational for the Gregs to scrap it, during its useful life. In any event, to have shifted over to steam power at any stage in the nineteenth century would have rendered the mill uncompetitive. This is because distance from the coalfield would have increased transport costs. The choice for the Gregs at Styal was, therefore, between water power or closure. The former was workable, the latter unthinkable.

The declining fortunes of Quarry Bank Mill during the late nineteenth century and the inter-war period mirror the experience of many mills founded during the industrial revolution. At a time when Britain's premier export industry was feeling the draught of foreign competition, mills such as Quarry Bank were in a poor position to respond to change. Archaic buildings, unsuitable for new machinery, continued to be used whilst any sort of return, however meagre, could be reaped. The position of the mill at the centre of the community meant that its life was even further prolonged. Its revitalisation as a museum in 1978 and its subsequent development are the products of post-industrial society. Greater leisure and burgeoning interest in the past have helped to guarantee its success.

NOTES

1 The cotton industry in the eighteenth century

1 D. Defoe, *A tour of the whole island of Great Britain* (first published 1724–6), Penguin edn, p. 69.
2 *Ibid.*, pp. 105, 370.
3 A. P. Wadsworth and J. de Lacy Mann, *The cotton trade and industrial Lancashire 1600–1780* (Manchester 1931), pp. 4–5.
4 *Ibid.*, pp. 12–13.
5 *Ibid.*, pp. 24–5.
6 *Ibid.*, p. 115.
7 E. Baines, *History of Liverpool* (Liverpool 1835), p. 302.
8 D. C. Coleman, *The domestic system in industry* (London 1967), pp. 4–7.
9 G. W. Daniels, *The early English cotton industry* (Manchester 1920), pp. 35–6.
10 R. Guest, *A compendious history of cotton manufacture* (London 1823), p. 10.
11 G. W. Daniels, *The early English cotton . . .* , p. 35.
12 W. Radcliffe, *Origin of power loom weaving* (Manchester 1829), p. 131.
13 Wadsworth and Mann, *The cotton trade . . .* , pp. 241–8.
14 *Ibid.*, p. 238.
15 *Ibid.*, pp. 224–40.
16 *Ibid.*, pp. 232–6.
17 D. Defoe, *Complete English tradesman* (Franklin Reprint 1970), p. 274.
18 Wadsworth and Mann, *The cotton trade . . .* , p. 295.
19 *Ibid.*, p. 42.
20 K. Honeyman, *Origins of enterprise* (Manchester 1982), p. 80.
21 M. M. Edwards, *The growth of the British cotton trade, 1780–1815* (Manchester 1967), p. 3.
22 Wadsworth and Mann, *The cotton trade . . .* , p. 415.
23 *Ibid.*, p. 415.
24 G. W. Daniels, *The early English cotton . . .* , pp. 78–83, 113–17.
25 S. D. Chapman, *The cotton industry in the Industrial Revolution* (London 1972), p. 30.
26 *Second annual report of the Poor Law commissioners*, Parliamentary Papers 1836 (595) XXIX, Part I, p. 414.
27 S. D. Chapman, *The cotton industry . . .* , pp. 156–64.
28 E. Penrose, *The theory of the growth of the firm* (Oxford 1959), p. 6.
29 S. Pollard, *The genesis of modern management* (London 1965), pp. 1–24.

30 *Ibid.*, pp. 39–47; Wadsworth and Mann, *The cotton trade . . .* , p. 90.
31 Wadsworth and Mann, *The cotton trade . . .* , p. 407. Recent research of my own into the parish apprentice registers of London parishes suggest the practice was very widespread.
32 D. Roberts, *Paternalism in early Victorian England* (London 1979), pp. 171–83.
33 P. Mathias, *The transformation of England* (London 1979), p. 102.
34 S. Pollard, 'Fixed capital in the industrial revolution in Britain', *JEH* 23 (1964), p. 300.
35 S. D. Chapman, 'Fixed capital formation in the British cotton industry', *EcHR* 23 (1970), p. 249.
36 R. H. Tawney, *Religion and the rise of capitalism* (London 1936); M. Weber, *The Protestant ethic and the spirit of capitalism* (London 1930); other major contributions to the Nonconformity debate may be found in R. W. Green, *Protestantism and Capitalism* (Boston 1959).
37 P. L. Payne, 'Industrial entrepreneurship and management in Great Britain', in eds. M. M. Postan and P. Mathias, *Cambridge Economic History of Europe*, Vol. VII, Part I (Cambridge 1978), p. 182.

2 Samuel Greg and Quarry Bank Mill, 1783–1815

1 R. P. Greg, 'The genealogical history of the family of Greg', p. 31 (MS microfilmed by MCL by kind permission of Mr A. C. Greg).
2 *Ibid.*, pp. 9–14, 101.
3 *Ibid.*, p. 14.
4 *Ibid.*, pp. 29–32.
5 Little is known about Robert Hamilton, but it is likely that he was Robert Hyde's brother-in-law.
6 R. P. Greg, 'The genealogical history . . .', p. 30.
7 M. B. Rose, 'The Gregs of Styal, 1750–1914: the emergence and development of a family business' (unpublished PhD thesis, Manchester 1977), p. 209.
8 R. P. Greg, 'The genealogical history . . .', p. 29.
9 *Ibid.*, p. 32.
10 R. H. Greg, 'Memoranda of Greg concerns 1784–1867' (MS), p. 31.
11 R. P. Greg, 'The genealogical history . . .', p. 220.
12 *Ibid.*, p. 40. Further details of these families can be found in Wadsworth and Mann, *'The cotton trade . . .'* for the Philipses see pp. 288–301; the Heywoods, p. 40, and the Hibberts, p. 231. It is not known if the Hydes themselves were Nonconformists, but they were in contact with many who were.
13 A. Thackray, 'National knowledge in cultural context: the Manchester model', *AHR* 32 (1974), p. 680.
14 As, for example, in a letter from Hannah Greg to Elizabeth Greg, 21 May 1816.
15 M. R. Audubon (ed.), *Audubon and his journals* (London 1898), pp. 134–5.
16 Catherine Stanley's view of the Gregs, quoted in John Morley, 'William Rathbone Greg: a sketch', in *Critical miscellanies*, Vol. III (London 1886), p. 219.
17 *Ibid.*, p. 220.
18 R. H. Greg, 'Memoranda of Greg concerns, 1750–1867', p. 114.

19 R. P. Greg, 'The genealogical history . . . ', p. 33.
20 R. H. Greg, 'Memoranda of Greg . . . ', p. 27.
21 See above, Chapter 1.
22 Quarry Bank memoranda in possession of Mr W. Salt, Styal, Cheshire.
23 M. M. Edwards, *The growth of the British* . . . , p. 11.
24 G. W. Daniels, *The early English cotton* . . . , pp. 105–10.
25 R. P. Greg, 'The genealogical history . . . ', p. 217.
26 That Greg did not think of himself as a cotton spinner is illustrated in a
    lease with the Earl of Stamford in 1790 (REM. 4252 in John Rylands Library,
    Manchester), when he gave his occupation as 'merchant'.
27 S. D. Chapman, *The early factory masters* (Newton Abbot 1967), p. 128.
28 MCL C5/15/1, Quarry Bank wages book, 1790.
29 R. H. Greg 'Memoranda of Greg . . . ', p. 2.
30 N. S. Buck, *The development of the organization of Anglo-American trade,*
    1800–50 (Yale 1925), p. 33.
31 MCL C5/1/9/2, Quarry Bank cash book 1791–7.
32 JRL REM 4240, 27 July 1790, lease between Samuel Greg and Lord
    Stamford; Samuel Greg and Matthew Fawkner (John Rylands Library,
    Manchester); REM 4253, 27 July 1790, lease between Samuel Greg and Lord
    Stamford. See below, Section III for a discussion of labour supply; the Styal
    factory colony is discussed in Chapter 6.
33 Samuel Greg's valuation of Quarry Bank, 1796.
34 See below, Section III.
35 Payments for hand-loom weaving at Styal appear in MCL C5/1/9, cash
    book, 1787–90.
36 MCL M8/1/1, 'Proceedings of the Society of Merchants trading on the
    continent of Europe, 1794–6', p. 45.
37 M. M. Edwards, *The growth of the British* . . . , pp. 11–12.
38 *An account of the cotton and woollen mills and factories in the United Kingdom of*
    Great Britain and Ireland, 1803–18, House of Lords Sessional Papers, Vol.
    CVIII, 1819, 66.
39 'Memoranda of Greg concerns, 1750–1867', p. 23.
40 R. P. Greg, 'The genealogical history . . . ', p. 37.
41 For a detailed account of fluctuations in the cotton trade during the
    Napoleonic Wars, see M. M. Edwards, *The growth of the British* . . . ,
    pp. 12–24.
42 I am grateful to Mr S. Graham for explaining the archaeological evidence at
    Styal to me.
43 W. C. Henry, *A biographical note of the late Peter Ewart* (Manchester 1844),
    p. 7.
44 MCL C5/1/2/1, partnership accounts.
45 MCL C5/1/2/2, Samuel Greg's personal account.
46 *Ibid.*
47 *Ibid.*, see below Chapter 6 for details of the factory colony.
48 'Memoranda of Greg concerns, 1750–1867', p. 23; MCL F.67 C.38, statistics
    obtained in Samuel Crompton's spindlage census, 1811.
49 MCL C5/1/2/2, Samuel Greg's personal account.
50 *Ibid.*
51 'Memoranda of Greg concerns, 1750–1867', pp. 108, 112.
52 M. B. Rose, 'The role of the family . . . ', *BH* 19 (1977), p. 30; the price index

rose by 84 per cent between 1780–4 and 1810–14: B. Mitchell and P. Deane, *Abstract of British historical statistics* (Cambridge 1962), pp. 468–9.

53 S. Pollard, 'Labour in Great Britain', in eds. P. Mathias and M. M. Postan, *The Cambridge Economic History of Europe*, Vol. VII, Part I (Cambridge 1978), p. 102.

54 R. D. Lee and R. S. Schofield, 'British population in the eighteenth century', in eds. R. Floud and D. N. McCloskey, *The Economic History of Britain since 1700*, Vol. I (Cambridge 1981), pp. 17–35.

55 S. Pollard, 'Labour in Great Britain . . .', p. 148.

56 W. Lazenby, 'The economic and social history of Styal, 1750–1850' (unpublished MA thesis, University of Manchester 1949), pp. 12–13.

57 V. A. C. Gatrell, 'Labour, power and the size of firms in Lancashire cotton in the second quarter of the nineteenth century', *EcHR* 30 (1977), p. 98.

58 MCL C5/1/1/3, valuation of Quarry Bank Mill by John Kennedy and Peter Ewart.

59 J. Dunlop and R. D. Denman, *English apprenticeship and child labour: a history* (London 1912), p. 70.

60 G. Nicholls, *History of the English Poor Law* (London 1898), pp. 94–6.

61 R. Burns, *History of the Poor Laws* (London 1764), p. 212.

62 *Nottingham Journal*, 14 January 1775.

63 *Wheeler's Manchester Chronicle*, 8 January 1785; a survey of provincial newspapers of the manufacturing districts for 1775–90 has shown that these were by no means isolated examples.

64 Details can be found in my unpublished article entitled 'The pauper apprenticeship system 1780–1834'; S. D. Chapman, *The early factory . . .*, pp. 169–71.

65 See below for details of the Gregs' Medical Officer; S. D. Chapman, *The early factory . . .*, p. 173.

66 Extract from a typical apprentice indenture.

67 See below, Chapter 6, for details of treatment of parish apprentices.

68 JRL REM 4240, 27 July 1970, lease between Lord Stamford, Samuel Greg and Matthew Fawkner.

69 MCL, Quarry Bank collection of apprentice indentures.

70 MCL C5/8/9/1, February 1817, letter from the Vicar of Biddulph to Samuel Greg.

71 MCL C5/8/9/2, February 1817, letter from Samuel Greg to the Vicar of Biddulph.

72 *Report on the state of children employed in cotton mills and factories*, PP 1816 (397) III, p. 374.

73 Registers of Apprenticeship, St Luke's Chelsea, 1791–1842; St Pancras 1790–1834, (both Greater London Record Office), St Martin-in-the-Fields (Westminster City Record Office); *Report from the committee on the bill to regulate the labour of children in the mills and factories of the United Kingdom*, PP 1831–2 (706) xv, evidence of Charles Aberdeen; A. Redford, *Labour migration in England 1800–50* (Manchester 1964), p. 26.

74 MCL C5/8/9/5, evidence of Thomas Priestley.

75 MCL MF 743, Quarry Bank medical records; MCL C5/1/15/2–5, wages books; PRO HO 107/115, 1841 Census Enumerators' Book for the township of Pownall Fee; Cheshire Record Office, Census Enumerators' Book, 1851.

76 MCL C5/5/1, workers' agreements.

77 MCL C5/5/5, workers' agreements.
78 See below, Chapter 6, for further discussion of wage rates.
79 See N. S. Buck, *The development of the organization* . . . , pp. 4–30, for a discussion of the difference between merchants and agents.
80 MCL C5/1/2/1, Chancery Lane stock accounts.
81 *Ibid.*
82 *Ibid.*
83 *Ibid.*
84 *Ibid.*
85 'Memoranda of Greg concerns, 1750–1867', p. 29.
86 *Ibid.*, p. 7.
87 M. B. Rose, 'The Gregs of Styal . . . ' (unpublished PhD thesis, University of Manchester 1977), p. 225.
88 'Memoranda of Greg concerns 1750–1867', p. 28.
89 M. M. Edwards, *The growth of the British Cotton* . . . , p. 178.

3 Expansion, 1815–1834

1 D. A. Farnie, *The English cotton industry and the world market* (Oxford 1979), p. 23.
2 B. R. Mitchell and P. Deane, *Abstract* . . . (Cambridge 1962), p. 491.
3 D. A. Farnie, *The English cotton* . . . , p. 9.
4 B. R. Mitchell and P. Deane, *Abstract* . . . , p. 491; A. D. Gayer, W. W. Rostow and A. J. Schwartz, *The growth and fluctuation of the British economy 1790–1850* (Brighton 1975), p. 155.
5 D. C. L. Pares collection 4 March 1819, letter from Isaac Hodgson to Thomas Pares.
6 MCL C5/6/5, ledger relating to the affairs of Quarry Bank.
7 Quoted R. L. Hills, *Power in the industrial revolution* (Manchester 1970), p. 109.
8 See below, Section IV.
9 See above Chapter 2 for details.
10 'Memoranda of Greg concerns 1750–1867', p. 16.
11 MCL C5/1/2/5, Caton machinery and building accounts.
12 *Ibid.*
13 MCL C5/1/2/6, partnership accounts; LCP PL 2/12, plan of the Gregs' Lancaster mill 1849; *First report . . . employment of children* . . . , PP 1833 (450) xx, pp. 34–5.
14 *Supplementary reports . . . employment of children* . . . , Part II, PP 1834 (167) xx, p. 145; MCL C5/1/2/6, partnership accounts; 'Memoranda of Greg concerns 1750–1867', p. 37.
15 *Ibid.*
16 MCL C5/1/2/6, partnership accounts; B. R. Mitchell and P. Deane, *Abstract* . . . , p. 179.
17 T. Ellison, *The cotton trade of Great Britain* (Liverpool 1886), p. 68.
18 V. A. C. Gatrell, 'Labour, power and the size of firms in Lancashire cotton in the second quarter of the nineteenth century', 181EcHR 30 (1977), pp. 95–139; R. Lloyd-Jones and A. A. LeRoux, 'The size of firms in the cotton industry: Manchester 1815–41', *EcHR* 33 (1980), pp. 72–82.
19 Details concerning the linen trade in Barnsley and Norwich can be found in

W. G. Rimmer, *Marshalls of Leeds, flax-spinners 1788–1886* (Cambridge 1960), pp. 126–8 and J. Clapham, 'Transference of the worsted industry from Norfolk to the West Riding', *EJ* 20 (1910), p. 197.

20 B. R. Mitchell and P. Deane, *Abstract . . .* , p. 201; W. G. Rimmer, *Marshalls of Leeds*, p. 127.

21 MCL C5/8/12, 14 May 1829, letter from Robert Hyde Greg to Samuel Greg.

22 *Ibid.*; this is confirmed by data, admittedly patchy, contained in *Select committee on manufacturers, shipping and commerce*, PP 1833 (690) v, evidence of J. Milne.

23 L. Hannah, *The rise of the corporate economy* (London 1976), p. 11; S. R. H. Jones, 'Price associations and competition in the British pin industry, 1814–40', *EcHR* 26 (1973).

24 M. M. Edwards, *The growth of . . .* , pp. 139–42.

25 MCL C5/1/2/2, Henshall's valuation of water power, 1849; MCL C5/3/1, Quarry Bank memoranda, p. 42.

26 A. E. Musson, 'Industrial motive power in the United Kingdom, 1800–70', *EcHR* 29 (1976), p. 420.

27 MCL C5/8/6, disputes over damming the River Bollin.

28 *Ibid.*

29 Much greater detail of this expenditure can be found in M. B. Rose, 'The Gregs of Styal . . .' , pp. 30–2, 60–4, 71–4. The difference between the level of expenditure given here and the valuation of fixed capital shown in Table 3.2 is explained by depreciation.

30 MCL C5/1/2/3, partnership accounts.

31 MCL C5/1/2/4, partnership accounts.

32 S. D. Chapman, 'Financial constraints on the growth of firms', *EcHR* 32 (1979), pp. 50–69.

33 MCL C5/1/2/2–3, partnership accounts.

34 MCL C5/1/2/3, partnership accounts.

35 MCL C5/1/2/6, partnership accounts.

36 See above, Chapter 2.

37 MCL C5/1/2/6, partnership accounts.

38 LUL (Rathbone collection), letter from Hannah Greg to Elizabeth Rathbone, 21 May 1816.

39 R. H. Greg, 'Travel journal' (MS in possession of Mr A. C. Greg).

40 *Ibid.*

41 *Ibid.*

42 Samuel Greg's eldest son, Thomas, had been all but adopted by his uncle and was being trained in marine insurance; MCL C5/1/2/4, partnership accounts.

43 MCL C5/1/2/4, partnership accounts.

44 *Ibid.*

45 *Ibid.*

46 R. Burn, *Statistics of the cotton trade* (Manchester 1847), p. 25.

47 R. C. O. Matthews, *A study of trade cycle history* (Cambridge 1954), p. 129; *Select committee on manufacturers . . .* , PP 1833 (690) v, p. 35.

48 MCL C5/8/12, 14 May 1929, letter from Robert Hyde Greg to Samuel Greg.

49 MCL C5/1/2/4, partnership accounts.

50 *Ibid.*; it should be noted that returns consist of profit plus interest on partners' capital plus the rent paid to Samuel Greg.

51 MCL C5/8/12, 14 May 1829, letter from Robert Hyde Greg to Samuel Greg.
52 *Ibid.*
53 MCL C5/1/1/3, valuation of Quarry Bank Mill by John Kennedy and Peter Ewart, 1831–2.
54 MCL C5/8/1/16, 20 August 1829, letter from Robert Hyde Greg to Samuel Greg.
55 Quarry Bank memoranda 1784–1850 (by kind permission of Mr W. Salt).
56 MCL C5/1/2/6, partnership accounts.
57 *Ibid.*
58 D. Bythell, *The handloom weavers* (Cambridge 1969), p. 76.
59 QB 30 August 1833, letter from Samuel Greg Senior to Robert Hyde Greg.
60 *Ibid.*
61 J. Morley, 'William Rathbone Greg: a sketch', in *Critical miscellanies*, vol. III (London 1886).
62 MCL, 15 May 1833, William Rathbone Greg and Elizabeth Rathbone.
63 MCL C5/1/15/2, wages book.
64 *Report on the state of children* . . . , PP 1816 (397) III, p. 374; MCL C5/1/15/2, wages book. See below Chapters 4 and 6 for details of the Bollington mill.
65 *Supplementary reports . . . employment of children* . . . , Part II, PP 1834 (253) xx.
66 B. L. Hutchins and A. Harrison, *A history of factory legislation* (3rd edn, London 1966), p. 9.
67 42 Geo III C. 73, *The health and morals of apprentices Act.*
68 *An account of the cotton and woollen mills and factories in the United Kingdom of Great Britain and Ireland 1803–18*, House of Lords sessional papers, Vol. CVIII, 1819, 66.
69 Registers of Apprenticeship for St Luke's Chelsea (Greater London Record Office); St Martin-in-the-Fields (Westminster City Record Office) and St Botolph-without-Aldersgate (Guildhall).
70 *Report on the state of children* . . . , PP 1816 (397) III, p. 133.
71 See below Chapter 6 for further details.
72 QB, Quarry Bank memoranda.
73 *Select committee on manufacturers* . . . PP 1833 (690) VI, p. 680.
74 See below Chapter 4 for discussion of the ending of the parish apprentice system and for the reduction of labour turnover at Quarry Bank.
75 'Memoranda of Greg concerns 1750–1867', p. 42.
76 *Ibid.*, pp. 42–5.
77 L. Faucher, *Manchester in 1844* (Manchester 1844), p. 96.
78 R. Boyson, *The Ashworth Cotton enterprise* (Oxford 1970), p. 18.
79 A. Smith, *The theory of moral sentiments* (London 1759) quoted by H. Perkin, *The origins of modern English society, 1780–1880* (London 1969), p. 85 and T. Malthus quoted *ibid.*, p. 89.
80 *Ibid.*, p. 38.
81 *Ibid.*, p. 88; 'Industrial capital and landed investment: the Arkwrights in Herefordshire 1809–43', in E. L. Jones and G. E. Mingay (eds.), *Land, labour and population in the industrial revolution* (London 1967).
82 R. G. Wilson, 'The Denisons and Milnes: eighteenth century merchant landowners', in eds. J. T. Ward and R. G. Wilson, *Land and industry* (Newton Abbot 1971), pp. 147–8, 158–9.
83 See above Chapter 2; a much more detailed discussion of this issue can be

found in M. B. Rose, 'Diversification of investment by the Greg Family 1800–1914', *BH* 21 (1979), pp. 79–96.

4 The middle years, 1834–1870

1 C. H. Lee, 'The cotton textile industry', in ed. R. Church, *The dynamics of Victorian business* (London 1980), p. 162.
2 D. A. Farnie, *The English cotton* . . . , p. 136.
3 C. H. Lee, The cotton textile . . . , p. 161.
4 QB, engineer's plans 1836; MCL C5/1/4/3 mill ledger; QB, plan of Quarry Bank Mill 1844.
5 Quarry Bank memoranda 1784–1850.
6 *Lancaster Guardian*, December 1837; 'Memoranda of Greg concerns 1750–1867', p. 16.
7 *Lancaster Guardian*, December 1837.
8 'Memoranda of Greg concerns 1750–1867', p. 16. P. J. Gooderson, 'The economic and social history of Caton 1750–1914: a study of semi-industrial community' (unpublished MA thesis, University of Lancaster, 1969), p. 21.
9 'Memoranda of Greg concerns 1750–1867', p. 5.
10 Robert Hyde Greg, 'Journal'.
11 'Memoranda of Greg concerns 1750–1867'. See below Chapter 8.
12 *Ibid*.
13 QB, Greg scrapbook, obituary of Samuel Greg, Jr, 1876.
14 See below Chapter 6.
15 13 April 1850, letter from W. R. Greg to R. H. Greg, in possession of Mrs S. B. L. Jacks, Styal, Nr Wilmslow, Cheshire.
16 *Ibid*.
17 *Ibid*.
18 Quoted in prefatory memoir, edited by wife in W. R. Greg, *Enigmas of Life*.
19 MCL C5/1/3/2, water power at Quarry Bank, 1856.
20 MCL C5/1/2/8, partnership accounts; Bagshawe's History, Gazetteer and Directory of Derbyshire 1846; Vanessa Parker, 'Calver Mill Buildings', *Derbyshire Archaeological Journal* 39 (1963), p. 37.
21 'Memoranda of Greg concerns 1750–1867', p. 48.
22 MCL C5/1/2/8, partnership accounts.
23 Unfortunately it is not possible to undertake similar analyses at Calver and Reddish since documentation is inadequate; see below Chapter 5 for further discussion of productivity.
24 The most thorough analyses of the so-called 'cotton famine' can be found in D. A. Farnie, *The English cotton* . . . , pp. 135–71 and E. Brady, 'A reconsideration of the Lancashire cotton famine', *Agricultural History* 44 (1963), pp. 156–62.
25 QB 30 May 1861, letter from Robert Hyde Greg to Robert Philips Greg.
26 MCL C5/1/2/8, partnership accounts.
27 QB, 16 January 1861 letter from Robert Hyde Greg to Robert Philips Greg.
28 QB 8 August 1861, letter from Robert Hyde Greg to Robert Philips Greg.
29 QB 14 September 1862, letter from Robert Hyde Greg to Robert Philips Greg.
30 MCL C5/1/2/8, partnership accounts.
31 QB 10 October 1864, letter from Robert Hyde Greg to Robert Philips Greg.

32 G. N. von Tunzelmann, *Steam power and British industrialization to 1860* (Oxford 1978), pp. 132–3.
33 QB 29 May 1853, letter from Robert Hyde Greg to Robert Philips Greg.
34 A. J. Taylor, 'Concentration and specialization in the Lancashire cotton industry', *EcHR* 1 (1949), pp. 112–17.
35 QB 19 May 1856, letter from Robert Hyde Greg to Robert Philips Greg.
36 QB, undated letter from Mary Greg to Robert Philips Greg.
37 QB 29 March 1856, letter from Robert Hyde Greg to Robert Philips Greg.
38 QB 8 March 1856, letter from Robert Hyde Greg to Robert Philips Greg.
39 *First annual report of the Poor Law commissioners*, PP 1835 (500) xxxv, p. 212; letter from Robert Hyde Greg to Edwin Chadwick.
40 *Ibid.*, p. 212; letter from Edmund Ashworth to Edwin Chadwick.
41 *Second annual report of the Poor Law commissioners*, PP 1836 (595) xxix, p. 412.
42 *Report from the select committee of the House of Lords on the burdens affecting real property*, PP 1846 (411) vi, Part i, p. 376.
43 *First annual report of the Poor Law commissioners*, PP 1835 (500) xxxv, p. 220; 16 July 1835 letter from Robert Hyde Greg.
44 *Report . . . on the burdens affecting real property*, PP 1846 (411) vi, Part i, p. 376; MCL C5/1/15/2, wages book 1835.
45 CRO CRO/19/7 1861. Census Enumerators' Book for the township of Pownall Fee.
46 *Report . . . on the burdens affecting real property*, PP 1846 (411) vi, Part i, p. 376.
47 *Children's employment commission*, PP 1843 (210) xiv, pp. 211–12.
48 R. H. Greg, *The factory question* (London 1837); Anon., *Misrepresentations exposed in a letter addressed to Lord Ashley containing strictures on the letters on the Factory Acts as it affects the cotton manufacturers* (Manchester 1838).
49 PRO HO.107/115 1841, Census Enumerators' Book; CRO 1851–71, Census Enumerators' Book; see M. B. Rose, 'The Gregs of Styal . . .', p. 128 for further details.
50 See below Chapter 6 for a discussion of paternalism at Styal.
51 MCL C5/1/15/2–11, wages books.
52 See above Chapters 2 and 3.
53 QB 14 January 1861, letter from Robert Hyde Greg to Robert Philips Greg.
54 MCL C5/1/2/8, partnership accounts; Greg Brothers' accounts 1865–1903.
55 QB 19 May 1856, letter from Robert Hyde Greg to Robert Philips Greg.
56 *Ibid.*
57 *Ibid.*
58 See below Chapter 7.
59 M. B. Rose, 'Diversification . . .', *BH* 21 (1979), p. 108; CRO, will of Samuel Greg proved 22 July 1834; R. P. Greg, 'The genealogical history . . .', p. 27.
60 MCL C5/6/3/1, R. H. Greg ledger; abstract of a Deed of Title for Reddish Estate, 1938.
61 MCL C5/8/7/18 2 September 1829, letter from Robert Hyde Greg to Samuel Greg.
62 MCL C5/8/7/19 11 July 1829, letter from Robert Hyde Greg to Samuel Greg.
63 M. B. Rose, 'Diversification . . .', *BH* 21 (1979), p. 83.

5 The later Gregs, 1870–1914

1 D. Landes, *The unbound Prometheus* (Cambridge 1969) pp. 231–58; D. H.

Aldcroft, 'The entrepreneur and the British economy 1870–1914', *EcHR* 16 (1964), pp. 116–18 and 121–3.

2 L. Sandberg, *Lancashire in decline* (Ohio 1974), pp. 15–93.

3 D. A. Farnie, *The English cotton . . .* , p. 171.

4 R. Robson, *The cotton industry in Britain* (London 1957), p. 331.

5 R. Tyson, 'The cotton industry', in ed. D. H. Aldcroft, *The development of British industry and foreign competition, 1875–1914* (London 1968), p. 100.

6 *Ibid.*, pp. 106–13.

7 *Ibid.*, p. 103.

8 R. Robson, *The cotton industry . . .* , p. 3.

9 Stockport Library, MS of A. Burton, 'A history of the parish of Wilmslow' (1872), p. 64.

10 MCL C5/1/2/8 partnership accounts.

11 MCL C5/1/3, Quarry Bank transfer book.

11 Quarry Bank memoranda.

12 LCL 920 MEL 32, Vol. xxvi, 28 May 1887, letter from Edward Hyde Greg to George Melly.

13 LCL 920 MEL 32, Vol. xxvi, 24 September 1888, letter from Edward Hyde Greg to George Melly.

14 D. Landes, *The Unbound . . .* , pp. 231–358; for further discussion of this issue, see later in this chapter when analysis of the Northrop looms is included.

15 L. Sandberg, *Lancashire . . .* , pp. 15–49.

16 Probate register, district probate registry.

17 MCL C5/1/3, Quarry Bank transfer book.

18 26 January 1884, letter from Edward Hyde Greg, Jr to Edward Hyde Greg (in possession of Mr A. C. Greg).

19 MCL C5/1/7/3, weaving production accounts.

20 L. Sandberg, *Lancashire . . .* , pp. 67–8.

21 W. Lazonick, 'Factor costs and the diffusion of ring spinning in Britain prior to World War I', *QJE* 56 (1981), p. 90.

22 L. Sandberg, *Lancashire . . .* , pp. 67–93.

23 MCL C5/1/7/3, weaving production accounts.

24 For further details of the life of H. P. Greg, see M. B. Rose, 'H. P. Greg' in *Dictionary of business biography*, Vol. ii (London 1985).

25 L. Sandberg, *Lancashire . . .* , p. 81.

26 *Ibid.*, p. 81.

27 A. Fowler, 'Trade unions and technical change: The automatic loom strike, 1908', Bulletin No. 6, *North West Group for the Study of Labour History, 1977*, pp. 43–55.

28 MCL C5/1/7/3, weaving production accounts. No reference to these strikes can be found in the *Cotton Factory Times*.

29 QB 23 March 1876, letter from Henry Russell Greg to Robert Philips Greg.

30 QB 7 July 1890, letter from Henry Russell Greg to Robert Philips Greg.

31 *Obituary of Henry Philips Greg*, published by R. Greg and Company Limited.

32 *Ibid.*

33 *Worrall's cotton spinners and manufacturers' directory 1884*; MCL C5/1/7/3, weaving production accounts; Cressbrook Mill letter book 1881–1908 (in possession of Mr W. Salt of Styal).

34 MCL C5/1/2/8, partnership accounts; Greg Brothers' accounts 1865–1903 (in possession of Mr W. Salt of Styal).
35 For a more detailed discussion of these two mills, see Mary B. Rose, 'The Gregs of Styal . . .' (unpublished PhD thesis, University of Manchester 1977), pp. 232–7.
36 D. H. Aldcroft, 'The entrepreneur . . .', *EcHR* 16 (1964), p. 128.

6 Paternalism and labour management

1 R. Bendix, *Work and authority in industry* (New York 1956), p. 16.
2 *Ibid.*
3 D. Roberts, *Paternalism in early Victorian England* (London 1979), p. 117.
4 J. Childs, *British management thought* (London 1969), p. 36.
5 R. Dore, *British factory, Japanese factory* (London 1973), pp. 269–75.
6 Quoted S. Pollard, 'The factory village in the industrial revolution', *EHR* 79 (1964), p. 527.
7 *Ibid.*, p. 528.
8 S. D. Chapman, *The early factory* . . . , p. 162.
9 S. Pollard, *The genesis of modern management* (London 1965), p. 192.
10 D. Roberts, *Paternalism in early* . . . , p. 180.
11 W. C. Taylor, *Notes of a tour in the manufacturing districts of Lancashire* (London 1842), p. 117.
12 R. Owen, *A new view of society* (Penguin edn 1970), p. 96.
13 E. Cadbury, *Experiments in industrial organization* (London 1912), p. xvii.
14 H. I. Dutton and J. E. King, 'The limits of paternalism', *Social History* 7 (1982), pp. 59–73.
15 See above Chapter 3.
16 R. H. Greg, *The factory question* (London 1836), p. 5.
17 MCL C5/8/9/15, the evidence of Thomas Priestley.
18 *Ibid.*
19 R. Owen, *A new view* . . . , p. 116.
20 MCL C5/1/9/1–2, Quarry Bank cash books, 1787–97.
21 LCL 920 MEL 28, Vol. xxII, 5358 28, December 1883, letter from Henry Russell Greg to George Melly.
22 MCL C5/1/7/1, apprentices' expenses.
23 W. Lazenby, *The economic and social* . . . , p. 113; MCL C5/1/4/3, Mill ledger 1835–8; PRO HO 107/115, 1841 Census Enumerators' Book for the township of Pownall Fee.
24 See above Chapters 2 and 3.
25 S. D. Chapman, *The early factory* . . . , p. 170.
26 MCL C5/5/2, apprenticeship indentures.
27 R. H. Greg, account of the Esther Price affair.
28 See above Chapter 3 and 4.
29 MCL C5/1/2/2–3, partnership accounts.
30 MCL C5/1/2/3–4, partnership accounts.
31 MCL C5/6/6, Styal estate ledger 1856–1914.
32 *Report from the select committee* . . . *on the burdens affecting real property*, PP 1846 (411) VI, Part I, p. 380.
33 PRO HO 107/115, 1851 Census Enumerators' Book for the township of Pownall Fee.

34 *Supplementary reports from the commissioners . . . relative to the employment of children*, Part I, PP 1834 (167) XIX, p. 204.
35 MCL C5/1/9/3, Quarry Bank cash book.
36 M. R. Audubon and E. Cones, *Audubon and his journals* (London 1897), p. 122.
37 CRO EUC 2/4/1, minutes of Norcliffe Chapel.
38 *Report of the select committee . . . on the burdens affecting real property*, PP 1846 (411) VI, p. 380.
39 P. M. Higginson, Sermon on the death of Mrs Ellen Melly (daughter of Samuel Greg), October 1894.
40 MCL C5/1/15/2–5, wages books, 1835–50.
41 Extract from American newspaper cutting in possession of Mrs S. B. L. Jacks, Styal, Nr Wilmslow, Cheshire.
42 F. Engels, *The condition of the working class in England* (Panther edn 1969), p. 214.
43 *Manchester Guardian*, 17 August 1842; MCL C5/1/7/2, production accounts.
44 H. I. Dutton and J. E. King, 'The limits of . . . ', p. 67; H. I. Dutton and J. E. King, *Ten per cent and no surrender* (Cambridge 1981), pp. 11–26.
45 See above Chapter 5.
46 Address given by H. P. Greg on the occasion of the opening of the club room at Styal, 8 November 1900.
47 *Ibid.*
48 Obituary of Henry Philips Greg.
49 Samuel Greg, *Two letters to Leonard Horner on the capabilities of the factory system* (London 1840) p. 6.
50 *Ibid.*, p. 17.
51 *Ibid.*, p. 24.
52 *Ibid.*, p. 16.
53 *Ibid.*, p. 17.
54 *Ibid.*, p. 10.
55 *Ibid.*
56 S. Greg, *A layman's legacy* (including a memoir by Dean Stanley) (London 1875) pp. 23–4.

7 Politics

1 For a detailed discussion of the position of industrialists in Victorian politics see W. L. Guttsman, *The British political elite* (London 1968), pp. 15–34, 167–95, and A. Howe, *The cotton masters 1830–60* (Oxford 1984).
2 H. Perkin, *The origins . . .*, pp. 38–42; M. Brock, *The great Reform Act* (London 1973), pp. 24–5.
3 E. Evans, *The forging of the modern state* (London 1983).
4 *Manchester Guardian*, September 1831.
5 *Manchester Guardian*, 7 September 1839; W. R. Greg, *Rocks ahead or the warnings of Cassandra* (London 1874), p. 42; W. R. Greg, 'Is popular judgement in politics more just than that of the higher orders?', *Nineteenth Century* 4 (1878), pp. 174–81.
6 MCL M87/4/2/8, Cobden papers; 11 May 1848, letter from William Rathbone Greg to Richard Cobden.
7 'Journal' of Robert Hyde Greg in possession of Mr and Mrs S. B. L. Jacks, Styal, Nr Wilmslow, Cheshire.

8 British Museum, Add MS 44371, Gladstone papers, W. R. Greg to W. E. Gladstone, 4 April 1852.
9 British Museum, Add MS 44372, Gladstone papers, W. R. Greg to W. E. Gladstone, 14 August 1852.
10 W. R. Greg, *Rocks ahead or the warnings . . .*, p. 5.
11 A. Howe, *The cotton masters . . .*, p. 235.
12 W. R. Greg, *An enquiry into the state of the manufacturing population and the causes and cures therein existing* (Manchester 1831).
13 *The Spectator*, 19 November 1881, obituary of William Rathbone Greg.
14 W. R. Greg, '*Mary Barton*: a tale of Manchester life', *Edinburgh Review* 89 (1849), p. 415.
15 N. McCord, *The Anti-Corn Law League* (London 1968); A. Prentice, *History of the Anti-Corn Law League* (new impression 1969), p. xviii; Lucy Brown, 'The Chartists and the Anti-Corn Law League', in ed. A. Briggs, *Chartist Studies* (London 1959).
16 MCL minute books of the Manchester Chamber of Commerce.
17 By far the most comprehensive account of the repeal of the Corn Laws is to be found in N. McCord, *The Anti-Corn . . .*
18 Quoted, *ibid.*, p. 25.
19 LUL Rathbone Papers, RP II.1.61, 6 March 1793, letter from Samuel Greg to William Rathbone.
20 MCL M8/2/1, Manchester Chamber of Commerce, minute book (by kind permission of the Manchester Chamber of Commerce), 19 February 1825, p. 309; obituary of Robert Hyde Greg, 26 February 1875, Country News Office, Cheshire.
21 QB, letter from Robert Hyde Greg to Robert Philips Greg, 1843.
22 *Anti-Corn Law circular*, 9 April 1840.
23 Robert Hyde Greg's 'Journal'.
24 *Ibid.*
25 *The League*, 18 November 1843.
26 MCL M20, Wilson papers, 1842, letter from Robert Hyde Greg to George Wilson.
27 W. D. Grampp, *The Manchester School of economics* (London 1960), p. 10.
28 *Anti-Bread Tax circular*, 24 February 1842.
29 W. R. Greg, *Agriculture and the Corn Law* (Manchester 1842); W. R. Greg, *Not over production but deficient consumption the source of our sufferings* (London 1842), pp. 8–9.
30 For a comprehensive list of W. R. Greg's publications, see M. B. Rose, 'The Gregs of Styal . . .' (unpublished PhD thesis, University of Manchester 1977), Appendix M.
31 MCL M8/1/1, 'Proceedings of the Society of Merchants trading on the continent of Europe, 1794–6', p. 45.
32 MCL M8/2/2, Manchester Chamber of Commerce, minute books, 1821–7, 8 November 1826, p. 456.
33 *Report from the select committee of the House of Lords on the burdens affecting real property*, PP 1846 (411) VI, Part I, p. 581.
34 See above Chapter 6 for details of this legislation.
35 59 Geo III c. 66.
36 3 and 4 Will IV c. 103.
37 P. Gaskell, *Artisans and machinery* (London 1836); P. Gaskell, *The manufac-*

turing population of England (London 1833); F. Engels, *The condition of the working class in England* (1st edn in Great Britain 1892); A. Ure, *The philosophy of manufactures* (London 1835); A. Ure, *The cotton manufacture of Great Britain,* 2 vols. (London 1836).

38 A. Howe, *The cotton masters . . .* , p. 183.

39 B. L. Hutchins and A. Harrison, *A history of . . .* , p. 62; 10 and 11 Vict c. 29.

40 R. H. Greg, *The factory question* (London 1837).

41 *Ibid.,* pp. 69–70.

42 Anon., *Misrepresentations exposed . . .*

43 National Association of factory occupiers, special report of the executive committee (Manchester 1855), p. 3.

44 *The Economist,* 14 January 1854 (in a letter from a cotton spinner). W. R. Greg was a regular contributor of unsigned pieces to *The Economist* at this time as a result of his close friendship with James Wilson, its editor. See E. J. Barrington, *The servant of all* (London 1929), Vol. I, p. 84. For a comprehensive discussion of the Preston strike see H. I. Dutton and J. E. King, *Ten per cent . . .*

45 See for example 'Proletariat on a false scent', *Quarterly Review* 132 (1872), pp. 251–94; 'Strikes, short hours, poor law and laissez-faire', *Fraser's Magazine* 86 (1872), pp. 265–81; *Mistaken aims and attainable ideals for the artisan class* (London 1876).

Epilogue

1 Letter written by Arthur Greg, 1915.

2 *Ibid.*

3 VAD diary of Madge Greg, by kind permission of Mr A. C. Greg.

4 R. Greg and Company Limited, prospectus.

5 W. A. Lewis, *Economic survey 1919–39* (London 1949), p. 56.

6 See above Chapter 5; W. Lazonick, 'Competition, specialisation and industrial decline', *JEH* 40 (1981), p. 31.

7 QB, wages books, 1914–39.

8 Letter dated 1936, Robert Alexander Greg to Alexander Carlton Greg, by kind permission of Mr A. C. Greg.

BIBLIOGRAPHY

MANUSCRIPT SOURCES

Libraries, museums, etc.
British Museum: Gladstone papers.
Cheshire Record Office: Census Enumerators' Books 1851–71; Norcliffe Collection.
Derby City Library: Pares Collection.
John Rylands Library: miscellaneous deeds.
Lancaster City Library: Greg Collection.
Liverpool City Library: Melly letters.
Liverpool University Library: Rathbone Collection.
Manchester Central Library: Greg Papers; Manchester Chamber of Commerce minute books; Anti-Corn Law letter books; R. P. Greg, 'The genealogical history and traditions of the family of Greg' (MS on microfilm consulted with the kind permission of Mr A. C. Greg).
Public Record Office: Census Enumerators' book 1841.
Quarry Bank Mill: miscellaneous letters, ledgers, plans etc.

Private collections
Mr A. C. Greg: 'Travel journal' of R. H. Greg; VAD diary of Madge Greg.
Mr and Mrs S. B. L. Jacks: 'Memoranda of Greg concerns 1750–1867' (MS of R. H. Greg); 'Journal' of R. H. Greg; miscellaneous letters.
Mr W. Salt: Cressbrook letter book; Quarry Bank memoranda 1784–1850.

PRINTED SOURCES

Books and articles published before 1900
Anon. *Misrepresentations exposed in a letter addressed to Lord Ashley containing strictures on the letters on the Factory Act as it affects the cotton manufacture* (Manchester 1838).
Audubon, M. R. (ed.) *Audubon and his journals* (London 1898).
Burn, R. *Statistics of the cotton trade* (Manchester 1847).
Burns, R. *History of the Poor Laws* (London 1764).
Defoe, D. *Complete English tradesman* (Franklin Reprint 1970).
  A tour of the whole island of Great Britain (first published 1724–6; Penguin edition).

Engels, F. *The condition of the working class in England* (Panther edn 1969).
Faucher, L. *Manchester in 1844* (Manchester 1844).
Gaskell, P. *The manufacturing population of England* (London 1833).
   Artisans and machinery (London 1836).
Greg, R. H. *The factory question* (London 1837).
Greg, S. *Two letters to Leonard Horner on the capabilities of the factory system* (London 1840).
   A layman's legacy (London 1875).
Greg, W. R. *An enquiry into the state of the manufacturing population and the causes and cures therein existing* (Manchester 1831).
   Agriculture and the corn law (Manchester 1842).
   Not over production but deficient consumption the source of our sufferings (London 1842).
   'Mary Barton: a tale of Manchester life', *Edinburgh Review* 89 (1849).
   Rocks ahead or the warnings of Cassandra (London 1874).
   'Is popular judgement in politics more just than that of the higher orders?', *Nineteenth Century* 4 (1878).
   Enigmas of life (London 1880).
Guest, R. *A compendious history of cotton manufacture* (London 1823).
Henry, W. C. *A biographical note of the late Peter Ewart* (Manchester 1844).
Morley, J. 'William Rathbone Greg: a sketch', in *Critical Miscellanies*, Vol. III (London 1886).
Nicholls, G. *History of the English Poor Law* (London 1898).
Owen, R. *A new view of society* (Penguin edition 1970).
Radcliffe, W. *Origin of power loom weaving* (Manchester 1829).
Ure, A. *The philosophy of manufactures* (London 1835).
   The cotton manufacture of Great Britain, 2 vols. (Manchester 1836).

Books and articles published since 1900
Aldcroft, D. H. 'The entrepreneur and the British economy, 1870–1914', *EcHR* 16 (1964).
   The development of British industry and foreign competition, 1875–1914 (London 1968).
Barrington, E. J. *The servant of all* (London 1929).
Bendix, R. *Work and authority in industry* (New York 1956).
Boyson, R. *The Ashworth cotton enterprise* (Oxford 1970).
Brady, E. 'A reconsideration of the Lancashire "cotton famine"', *Agricultural History* 44 (1963).
Buck, N. S. *The development of the organisation of Anglo-American trade 1800–50* (Yale 1925).
Bythell, D. *The handloom weavers* (Cambridge 1969).
Cadbury, E. *Experiments in industrial organisation* (London 1912).
Chapman, S. D. *The early factory masters* (Newton Abbot 1967).
   'Fixed capital formation in the British cotton industry', *EcHR* 23 (1970).
   The cotton industry in the industrial revolution (London 1972).
   'Financial constraints on the growth of firms', *EcHR* 32 (1979).
Child, J. *British management thought* (London 1969).
Church, R. (ed.) *The dynamics of Victorian business* (London 1980).
Clapham, J. 'Transference of the worsted industry from Norfolk to the West Riding', *EJ* 20 (1910).

Coleman, D. C. *The domestic system in industry* (London 1967).
Daniels, G. W. *The early English cotton industry* (Manchester 1920).
Dore, R. *British factory, Japanese factory* (London 1973).
Dunlop, J. and Denman, R. D. *English apprenticeship and child labour: a history* (London 1912).
Dutton, H. I. and King, J. E. *Ten per cent and no surrender* (Cambridge 1981).
'The limits of paternalism', *Social History* 7 (1982).
Edwards, M. M. *The growth of the British cotton trade 1780–1815* (Manchester 1967).
Evans, E. *The forging of the modern state* (London 1983).
Farnie, D. A. *The English cotton industry and the world market* (Oxford 1979).
Floud, R. and McCloskey, D. N. *The economic history of Britain since 1700*, Vol. I (Cambridge 1981).
Gatrell, V. A. C. 'Labour power and the size of firms in Lancashire cotton in the second quarter of the nineteenth century', *EcHR* 30 (1977).
Gayer, A. D., Rostow, W. W. and Schwartz, A. J. *The growth and fluctuation of the British economy 1790–1850* (Brighton 1975).
Grampp, W. D. *The Manchester School of Economics* (London 1960).
Green, R. W. *Protestantism and capitalism* (Boston 1959).
Guttsman, W. L. *The British political elite* (London 1967).
Hannah, L. *The rise of the corporate economy* (London 1976).
Hills, R. L. *Power in the industrial revolution* (Manchester 1970).
Honeyman, K. *Origins of enterprise* (Manchester 1982).
Howe, A. *The cotton masters 1830–60* (Oxford 1984).
Hutchins, B. L. and Harrison, A. *A history of factory legislation* (3rd edn, London 1966).
Jones, E. L. and Mingay, G. E. (eds.) *Land, labour and population in the industrial revolution* (London 1968).
Jones, S. R. H. 'Price associations and competition in the British pin industry 1814–40', *EcHR* 26 (1973).
Landes, D. *The unbound Prometheus* (Cambridge 1969).
Lazonick, W. 'Competition, specialisation and industrial decline', *JEH* 40 (1981).
'Factor costs and the diffusion of ring spinning in Britain prior to World War I', *QJE* 56 (1981).
Lewis, W. A. *Economic survey 1919–39* (London 1949).
Lloyd-Jones, R. and le Roux, A. A. 'The size of firms in the cotton industry: Manchester 1815–41', *EcHR* 33 (1980).
McCord, N. *The Anti-Corn Law League 1838–46* (London 1958).
Mathias, P. *The transformation of England* (London 1979).
Mathias, P. and Postan, M. M. (eds.) *Cambridge economic history of Europe*, Vol. VII, Part I (Cambridge 1978).
Matthews, R. C. O. *A study in trade cycle history* (Cambridge 1954).
Mitchell, B. R. and Deane, P. *Abstract of British historical statistics* (Cambridge 1962).
Musson, A. E. 'Industrial motive power in the United Kingdom 1800–70', *EcHR* 29 (1976).
Payne, P. L. 'Industrial entrepreneurship and management in Great Britain', in eds. M. M. Postan and P. Mathias, *Cambridge economic history of Europe*, Vol. VII, Part I (Cambridge 1978).

Penrose, E. *The theory of the growth of the firm* (Oxford 1959).
Perkin, H. *The origins of modern English society 1780–1880* (London 1969).
Pollard, S. 'The factory village in the industrial revolution', *EHR* 79 (1964).
'Fixed capital in the industrial revolution', *JEH* 23 (1964).
The genesis of modern management (London 1965).
'Labour in Great Britain', in eds. P. Mathias and M. M. Postan, *Cambridge economic history of Europe*, Vol. VII, Part I (Cambridge 1978).
Redford, A. *Labour migration in England 1800–50* (Manchester 1964).
Rimmer, W. G. *Marshalls of Leeds: flax spinners 1788–1886* (Cambridge 1960).
Roberts, D. *Paternalism in early Victorian England* (London 1979).
Robson, R. *The cotton industry in Britain* (London 1957).
Rose, M. B. 'The role of the family in the provision of capital and managerial talent in Samuel Greg and Company 1750–1840', *BH* 19 (1977).
'Diversification of investment by the Greg family 1800–1914', *BH* 21 (1979).
Sandberg, L. *Lancashire in decline* (Ohio 1974).
Tawney, R. H. *Religion and the rise of capitalism* (London 1936).
Taylor, A. J. 'Concentration and specialisation in Lancashire cotton industry', *EcHR* 1 (1949).
Thackray, A. 'Natural knowledge in cultural context: the Manchester model', *AHR* 32 (1974).
von Tunzelmann, G. N. *Steam power and British industrialisation to 1860* (Oxford 1978).
Wadsworth, A. P. and Mann, J. de Lacy. *The cotton trade and industrial Lancashire 1600–1780* (Manchester 1931).
Ward, J. T. and Wilson, R. G. (eds.) *Land and industry* (Newton Abbot 1971).
Weber, M. *The Protestant ethic and the spirit of capitalism* (London 1930).

Newspapers
Anti-Bread Tax Circular
Anti-Corn Law Circular
Lancaster Guardian
The League
Manchester Guardian
Nottingham Journal
The Economist
The Spectator
Wheeler's Manchester Chronicle

Parliamentary Papers
An account of the cotton and woollen mills and factories in the United Kingdom of Great Britain and Ireland 1803–18, House of Lords sessional papers, Vol. CVIII, 1819, 66.
Report on the state of children employed in cotton mills and factories, PP 1816 (397) III.
Report from the committee on the bill to regulate the labour of children in the mills and factories of the United Kingdom, PP 1831–2 (706) XV.
Select committee on manufactures, shipping and commerce, PP 1833 (690) V.
First report from the commissioners appointed to collect information in the manufacturing districts, relative to employment of children in factories, and as to the propriety and means of curtailing the hours of their labour, PP 1833 (450) XX.

Second report from the commissioners . . . relative to the employment of children . . . ,
PP 1833 (519) xx.
*Supplementary reports from the commissioners . . . relative to the employment of
children . . . ,* PP 1834 (167) xix; PP 1834 (253) xx.
First annual report of the Poor Law commissioners, PP 1835 (500) xxxv.
Second annual report of the Poor Law commissioners, PP 1836 (595) xxix, Part i.
Children's employment commission, PP 1843 (210) xiv.
*Report from the select committee of the House of Lords on the burdens affecting real
property,* PP 1846 (411) vi, Part i.

Unpublished theses
Gooderson, P. J. 'The economic and social history of Caton 1750–1914: a study
of a semi-industrial community', MA thesis, University of Lancaster,
1969.
Lane, J. 'Apprenticeship in Warwickshire 1700–1834', PhD thesis, University
of Birmingham, 1977.
Lazenby, W. 'The economic and social history of Styal 1750–1850', MA thesis,
University of Manchester, 1949.
Rose, M. B. 'The Gregs of Styal 1750–1914: the emergence and development of
a family business', PhD thesis, University of Manchester, 1977.

INDEX